MEGAPHYSICS III

NOTHING DOESN'T EXIST AND EVERYTHING DOES

DR. MITCHELL WICK

authorHOUSE®

AuthorHouse™
1663 Liberty Drive
Bloomington, IN 47403
www.authorhouse.com
Phone: 1 (800) 839-8640

Published by AuthorHouse 03/17/2017

ISBN: 978-1-5246-7436-6 (sc)
ISBN: 978-1-5246-7435-9 (e)

Print information available on the last page.

This book is printed on acid-free paper.

CONTENTS

FORWARD AND INTRODUCTION

Most individuals are aware of the "Big Bang" Theory about how 13.7 billion years ago a quantum bubble composed of 50% matter and 50% anti-matter exploded in a symmetrical 360 degree orb blast to form our universe. What most people don't realize or understand is the implications of the "Big Bang" ex nihilo or out of nothing. By definition and using math nothing(which is the absence of all properties)will and must remain nothing forever as mathematically nothing times infinity is still nothing, So as the quantum bubble is something and not nothing there must have been a catalyst if it was the first event. The catalyst is also something as something cannot be created out of nothing as nothing will always be nothing. Some theorists go even further saying that because our observable universe has no center of gravity or center of mass due to isotropism(observational symmetry)and homogeneity it also has no discernable edge. If these points are true then every point in this universe will have the exact same special relationship with every other point as the universe expands from Planck Length to 10^10 light years and beyond, a concept known as conformal space with regard to conformal mass and conformal time as in an inflation balloon which is part of Dr. Alan Guth's Inflation Theory Of course if this implies that there is nothing outside the quantum bubble that implies that EVERYTHING IS INSIDE THE QUANTUM BUBBLE INCLUDING SPACE AND TIME. This is an accepted viewpoint by many physicists but it is absolutely impossible! The Big Bang ex nihilo has to be false as well as any Inflation Theory ex nihilo as the only possible ex nihilo is the "nihilo ex nihilo" as nothing and only nothing can exist when there is only nothing in existence; and of course nothing is impossible or beyond the comprehension of mankind. This author will attempt to show what is illustrated in the previous book" What is the Dimension of Time?" that there were a near infinite number of completely parallel planes of space always existing as a container for contents(as a container can exist without contents and this isn't nothing as being a container is a property)and that the FIRST EVENT in the sequencing of events transformed these parallel planes into a vortex of primordial space-time(which is why space-time originally had a spiral configuration. It will show that using the fermionic state (vacuum state)transforming with rogue tachyons traveling below "c" turning them into bosons ;a time paradox formed oscillating time's arrow forward and backward causing a spin on the infinite number of planes which became a centrifuge effect forming the string dimensions and macroscopic dimensions as the intersection of two planes is a dimension and there were a near infinite number of parallel planes which were now curved by the time paradox oscillating forward with fermions and backwards with tachyons. This vortex with the string dimensions which were almost infinite as compactified dimensions became 26 compactified dimensions and then 11 or 10 whether or not super-gravity was included and the multiverse was formed. Recall that the space-time continuum by definition had no beginning or ending and therefore time always existed even before the first event although it was asymptotic to the value of infinity indicating infinite dilation or non-motion. This infinitely dilated time dimension wrapped around the infinite number of parallel planes to form the other dimensions in the spiral vortex model.

One should note that nothing plus infinity=infinity yet nothing cannot become infinity or everything without a catalyst and a catalyst is something. So in terms of logic {}+{everything}={everything} yet {}→{everything}if any only if

a catalyst acted upon →. $\left\{ \in \left| \sum_{-\infty}^{\infty} e^{-i\omega t} \right| \dfrac{0}{0} \right\}$ *As any catalyst*

is something represented by Δ let Δ = C then nothing or {} + Δ=

{everything} = $\left\{ \in \left| \sum_{-\infty}^{\infty} e^{-i\omega t} \left| \dfrac{0}{0} \right\} \right. - \Delta \right\}$ *as the catalyst Δ is part of*

everything and not part of nothing. nothing cannot form create or produce everything. Q. E. D. THIS IS WHY THE BIG BANG EX NI???

NIHILO IS NOT POSSIBLE UNDER ANY VIABLE PHYSICAL OR MATHEMATICAL LAWS RELATING TO QUANTUM MECHANICS, LOGIC, GROUP THEORY, QUANTUM FIELD THEORY, M THEORY OR RELATIVISTIC VARIANCE. THIS ONCE AGAIN REAFFIRMS THE BOUNDARY THAT NOTHING DOESN'T EXIST AS IF NOTHING DID EXIST IT STILL EXISTS AND WILL ALWAYS EXIST IN EXCLUSION OF EVERYTHING AND THAT WOULD MEAN THAT EVERYTHING DIDN'T EXIST AND DOESN'T EXIST WHICH IS A FALLACY.

CHAPTER ONE

THE NUMBER OF EIGENSTATES OF ENERGY IN THE MULTIVERSE

The Equation of Everything is a powerful mathematical tool. It shows that there are an infinite number of eigenstates going from n=0 to n=infinity yielding an infinite number of constants which are added to the tensor product yielding the total number of Riemannian Forces of Nature in curved Riemannian or Lorenzian Space-time. ¡ $(n)abcd = \Pi n = 0$ *to ¥ eigenstates of energy* 2^n +

$$\frac{1\pi\omega(i \rightarrow j)}{2^{n\pi\omega(j \rightarrow i)}} + 2\pi(R\,abc + or - \frac{1}{2R}\,gab \div +or - ih\Lambda ba\rho ab\ where$$

$\hbar = {}^h\overline{2\pi}$. R abc is the region of Euclidian Space plus or minus the region of of the space – time curvature metric acting from the Ricci Tensor R ab which is the inertial mass doinf the c???

Curving. Rab=$\hbar\rho$ *ab and the* wave *function* is + or -
i
ħ from the Schrodinger Equation so the denominator for the energy density of the wave

Function of all matter in the multiverse is +or -
i
ħΛbaρab as the energy density is heteropic (skipping between dimensions) which are Wick Rotated from Gian Carlo Wick's

math theory for incorporating dimensional flipping of eigenstates. Of course the 2π is flipped from $\hbar = \frac{h}{2\pi}$ is flipped into the numerator making a compactified form of the Equation of Everything Into a circle $C=2\pi R$ where the circumference is curved space-time=2π(Riemann forces of Nature) as the spiral operator over an infinite number of eigenstates

Net out as 0(zero) as the infinite product of $\frac{1}{2}$^$n\pi\omega$ $(j \rightarrow i) = 0$. All five String Theories or M theory compactify mathematically to a circle so this Equation of Everything describes String Theory(type IIA closed string theory) and describes M(Membraine) Theory. Of course there are 524,288 permutations to this equation of everything which are all added to the infinite number of eigen-states as described by the Spiral Operator acting on the function of angular momentum emerging from the initial to the final state and also the final state to the initial state as described by i=initial state and j=final state. In the case of n=0 which is the ground eigen-state $\frac{1}{2}$^0 π operating on an angular momentum ω of i(initial state) has an angular momentum of

$$\infty$$

The numerator is 2^$n+1\pi\omega$ which is also ∞. This produces the total number of eigenstates as $\frac{\infty}{\infty}$ which is everything except 0 as ∞ times $0 = 0$ which indicates that ∞ (nothing) = nothing so the total number of eigenstates in existance ever is everything except 0.

Therefore from the Equation of Everything which is a compactified form of M Theory proves conclusively that nothing doesn't exist and never existed or will exist. As a corollary to this axiom nothing can only result in nothing and to produce anything requires a catalyst Δ which isn't nothing.

CHAPTER TWO

BEFORE THE BIG BANG

There are several theories as to what caused the quantum bubble which is 50% matter and 50% anti-matter. One of which is the merging or collision of two membranes from disparate universes in the multiverse caused by the spin2vector Boson representing gravity. If a matter universe where gravity was positive and space-time curved inwardly merged with an anti-matter universe where space-time curved outwardly as in anti-gravity; the combination of the inward and outward curving of space-time in that region would cause an OSCILLATION OF SPACE-TIME IN WHICH THERE IS AN EXPANSION THEN CONTRACTION PHASE OF SPACE-TIME BETWEEN MATTER AND ANTI-MATTER FOLLOWED BY MATTER-ANTI-MATTER ANNHILATION WHICH RESULTED IN A SPIN OF A RECOMBINANT UNIVERSE ITNO A VORTEX WITH ANTI-MATTER AT ONE POLE AND MATTER AT THE OPPOSITE POLE WITH A FRACTURE NEAR THE CENTER WHICH IS THE SITE OF THE BIG BANG. THE ANTI-MATTER HAS MUTUAL REPULSION AS SHOWN MATHEMATICALLY IN MY BOOK 'MEGAPHYSICS II; AN EXPLANATION OF NATURE' AND THIS MUTUAL REPULSION OF ANTI-MATTER WITH OTHER ANTI-MATTER PUSHED THE MATTER IN THE QUANTUMBUBBLE OUTWARDLY WITH A TRAJECTORY OF 2πRADIANS OR *360* DEGREES IN AN ORB BLAST OF $6.75X10^{34}$ERG IN THE FIRST SECOND.

Again as previously mentioned in my book" Mega-physics II: An Explanation of Nature this is what caused the Big Bang, explains why there is so little anti-matter in this universe and what Dark Energy is. Also to form the quantum bubble there would have to have been a miniscule increment of matter exceeding the anti-matter so the curvature of space-time inward would exceed that outward or else the collsion of the two disparate multiverses would not have occurred.

Another theory which was previously noted was that there was a "Big Crunch" of another universe with the same space-time as our universe. In this case time dilated toward infinity constricting the space in this previous universe toward zero with actually reaching it as an asymptotic value, and of course as space-time IS A PERFECT FLUID this would have been a whirlpool effect or vortex downward as a current in the space-time of other universes involving the universe having the Big Crunch and causing ripples of space-time from other universes to rapidly approach the vortex of our universe just as the geometric expansion of our universe now is being pulled by space-time of other universes acting on our space-time while it's being pushed by dark energy from the repulsion of anti-particles with each other.

There is ONE OTHER POSSIBILITY AMONG MANY OTHERS WHICH MUST NOT BE DISMISSED REGARDING THE QUANTUM BUBBLE. IF THE QUANTUM BUBBLE HAD EVERYTHING IN IT AND WAS PART OF THE SPACE-TIME CONTINUUM IT WOULD HAVE ALWAYS BEEN THERE ALONG WITH THE SPACE AND TIME WAS DILATED TO INFINITY UNTIL 10^{-43}seconds after which was the Big Bang. Fermions and tachyons always existed in the near infinite number of parallel planes so why couldn't the quantum bubble have always existed. It may have been quiescent like a sebaceous cyst before it became infected then it reacted. This reaction would only occur if the 50:50 balance of anti-matter and matter were disturbed to which matter exceeded anti-matter. The boundary in this case would have to be so severe and absolute that it can never be breeched by ANYTHING. This is why the only TRUE BOUNDARY IS THAT OF SPACE-LESS-NESS AND IT IS IMPOSSIBLE OR BEYOND THE COMPREHENSION OF MANKIND. DOES THIS IDEA SATISFY OCCAM'S RAZOR?As space-time is a continuum and the quantum bubble was a continuum then the quantum bubble would have to have been a byproduct of space-time as there was nothing else. When space-time formed the string dimensions with the centrifuge effect with the time paradox discussed in the book "What is the Dimension of Time? "the quantum bubble could have been formed with the spin2 vector bosons forming from fermions and tachyons. Of course this WAS THE FIRST EVENT NOT THE BIG BANG. This would satisfy the requirement of this universe having no edge however the lack of a center of mass even in an isotropic universe would be hard to explain. Despite the fact that this is a simple explanation is it the simplest explanation or is the multiverse collision of two membranes where one universe was matter and one anti-matter? Is a Big Crunch of another universe with the same space-time as this universe be a simpler explanation? The law of conservation of energy would be conserved if the quantum bubble was always in existence as the potential energy would have been equal to the kinetic energy for an indeterminately long period of dilated time.

THE STEADY STATE THEORY WAS AN ACCEPTED IDEA PRIOR TO THE BIG BANG THEORY. It stated that galaxies stars and nebulae formed and were destroyed at the same rate as they were formed and until it was determined by Edwin Hubble in 1927 that the universe was expanding it was considered THE THEORY whereby space-time was infinite which is CORRECT. Of one considers the universe in which we exist is the only universe rather than the multi-verse then the sequencing of the first events are as follows:1)an infinite number of non-intersecting planes in the zero dimensional state with a confluence of D-0-Branes with fermions existing in the fermionic or vacuum state and tachyons existing above the speed of light. Fermions move one direction in time and tachyons in the opposite direction in time2). When rogue tachyons drop below the speed of light false boundary they cause a time paradox from the oscillation of the infinitely dilated or stopped time into a standing wave of time's arrow moving backwards and forwards forming a spin the a centrifuge effect with the formation of dimensions as the planes intersect each other and the fermions plus tachyons form spin 2 vector bosons representing gravity and anti-gravity.3) The initial space-time configuration was a vortex or a huge spiral with microscopic dimensions and strings gravitating toward the center. If the tachyons and bosons formed the Higgs Field at this time which is a vortex according to the tensor virial theorem and proof shown in this author's previous book "What is the Dimension of Time?" It is NOT IMPOSSIBLE THAT AT THIS TIME WERE THE EARLY FORMATIONS OF THE QUANTUM BUBBLE WITH matter and antimatter however it doesn't explain how matter and anti-matter were exactly 50:50 although the spin2 vector bosons may have curved space-time inward (matter) and outward(anti-matter)which would have made space-time in the quantum bubble initially as asymptotically flat while it situates in a huge spiral space-time while the quantum bubble had spin 2 vector bosons curving space-time equally inwardly and outwardly as anti-particles repel each other and particles attract each other as do particles and antiparticles resulting in self annihilation. Is this creation? 4)The formation of the string dimensions from an infinite number of parallel planes of space with an oscillating time paradox produce spin2 vector bosons which curve space by constricting and dilating time from the oscillation and may or may not have formed the quantum bubble from this. If this indicates creation of matter from energy then it may relate to the first event. Despite this there is soft evidence of a multiverse from CMB data from USC's Planck Team. There is a rotational vector in the quantum bubble as matter and antimatter spun and rotated gravitating to the poles before splitting in the center what this author always called the 0,0 point and in 19^{-43} seconds or Planck Time the mutual repulsion of all antiparticles pushed contained space in the quantum bubble (which is only a portion of the space in the infinite parallel planes)Still this would be the center of mass of this universe regardless of whether or not it was almost the first event. Despite the nearly isotropic quality of this universe there is most likely(according to Occam's Razor)a huge supermassive black hole approximately 16 to 30 billion light years away and would only be detected by perturbations in space-time curvature or gravity waves showing a progressive increase in the rotational vector of space-time. Note that eventhough the Big Bang occurred approximately 13.7 billion years ago light from the source of the Big Bang would be perturbed by different regions of space-time with different curvature metrics including at the event horizons of black holes so the distance is warped by the curvature of space-time near heavy masses rather than just relying on the cosmologic constant which is the energy density of a vacuum(space is not a vacuum due to the B.M.R. heating space by 2.74 degrees kelvin. Stating that universe has no edge is because all the measuring devices within the quantum bubble of this universe is limited in measurement to this universe and the measurements are skewed because the measuring device is part of what's being measured;a premise from Quantum Mechanics.

There must have been a "Big Bang " or Inflation otherwise there wouldn't be an Background Microwave Radiation assuming of course that there isn't an alternative explanation for the B.M.R. As there was indeed a "Big Bang " then space-time is inversely proportional to mass as the extreme curvature of the quantum bubble causes a severe constriction of space by severely dilated time in the presence of significantly large mass. If there are people that still feel that the "steady state "theory is still viable they would have to come up with an alternative explanation for the B.M.R. and the WOMP studies of our universe. Interestingly enough, Inflation as purported by Dr. Alan Guth fits a totally isotropic universe with no center of gravity or edge much more accurately than "The Big Bang" which would have canter of mass at the site of "The Big Bang" in an area of severely spiraling space-time which would either be Schwarzchild Space-time if it's a supermassive black hole or just a huge enveloping vortex in space-time is there is no more extant black hole event horizon. Again this can be determined by gravity waves as performed in the LIGO project measuring the extreme curvature of space-time going from near flatness to near infinite curvature as space-time constricts toward a point without reaching it. Inflation apparently allow the multiverse possibly in layers like unicellular organisms stacked up in the fluid of space-time and while there is an edge it is indiscernable from points on the inflating surface as the curvature of the surface appears to be continuous unless a singularity in space-time causes the balloon to tear and then pop causing a clearly discernable Big Crunch. In the "Steady State Theory " space-time must be a Harmonic Oscillator oscillating according to the vibrational frequency of strings and also electromagnetic radiation. Here matter is always being formed from simple matter(strings)to more complex matter(galaxies) and then broken down again to compounds, molecules, atoms, Hadrons and strings which vibrate and rotate in ways that space-time does. Here the first event must also be the Infinite Plane Theory propounded by this author in previous work "What is the Dimension of Time?" whereby Fermions and tachyons causing infinitely dilated time to oscillate then form standing waves then spin into a centrifuge effect with the intersection of planes causing the D-0-branes to form orbifolds of space-time of between 26 and an infinite number of dimensions from which inflation can occur. This can occur in Fock Space or Hilbert Space. Hilbert space must then be subdivided down into partitions like dots on a television screen. There is CMB data regarding Dark

Flow which implies the existence of the Multiverse as per the Planck Team at U.S.C. Please note that the steady- state theory is totally compatible with the multi-verse.(Pierpoli et al.,)and Dr. Laura Mersini-Houghton at Chapel Hill in North Carolina. The only problems with the Steady-State Theory are as follows:1) the existence of the Background Microwave Radiation reflects a Big Bang 2)the W.O.M.P. measurements of 1996 reflect a relative homogeneity with some clumping reflecting a 360 degree orb blast and finally 3)the expansion discovered by Edwin Hubble in 1927 reflects that the universe is expanding. In other ways the Steady State Theory holds water and blends very well with the infinite plane hypothesis. The problems with the Big Bang only relate to the singularity whereby space and time are universally self contained in the quantum bubble with nothing outside(which us clearly impossible) and that the universe has no edge or center of gravity(which breaks Isaac Newton's hypothesis that a mass of 10^{64} kg has a center of mass as does every mass including a photon. Also the Laws of Conservation of Energy, Conservation of the mass equivalent of energy and the law of conservation of dimensions are violated as dimensions were formed from parallel planes by the oscillating time paradox from tachyons and fermions into bosons. According to Quantum Mechanics with infinitely dilated time(time infinity or time stopped)the Probability that a rogue tachyon will slow down to the speed of light approaches 100 % and the backward time arrow at the speed of light from the rogue tachyon and forward time's arrow with the fermions caused the time paradox oscillation, standing waves, spin and centrifuge effect that formed the string dimensions and spiral space-time from the infinite parallel planes. Therefore this FIRST EVENT DID HAPPEN AND IT WAS THE FIRST EVENT FORMING THE MULTIVERSE OR OUR UNIVERSE PRE BIG BANG. Inflation is consistent with an isotropic homogeneous universe with no edge but certainly isn't consistent with everything everywhere being within the quantum bubble with nothing outside it either although again it allows for the multi-verse layered adjacent with regard to fluid space-time to other universes. Inflation clearly is pure expansion without rotation while The Big Bang must have had rotation maximized at the very first instant since the Big Crunch or collision of two or three membranes from the multi-verse pre Big Bang although the quantum bubble may have existed since the initial time paradox which transformed parallel planes into a vortex with spin2 vector bosons, In terms of the Equation of Everything that compactifies as String Theory to a circle the circumference of course is space-time curved by the angle from just above 0 to 2 pi radians. As a circle there is a hypothetical edge but as the sum of all positive and negative Riemann Forces of nature comprising the diameter never reach the circumference as space-time travels at 2.2x10^35(c)meters/sec the only occurrence of which the Riemann Forces of Nature reach the circumference is in a singularity such as a "Big Crunch" rip or tear in the fabric of fluid space-time at which time or occurrence a clear edge, interface or boundary is defined. Either way there is a CENTER OF MASS AND GRAVITY AT THE EXACT CENTER OF THE CIRCLE OR THE POINT OF THE DIAMATER WHERE THE POSITIVE AND NEGATIVE RIEMANN FORCES OF NATURE NET AS ZERO. This is an asymptotic value with regard to the five string theories but would in theory at least define the supermassive black hole which has the site of the Big Bang and MUST BE THE CENTER OF GRAVITY AND MASS OF THIS UNIVERSE FOR WHICH ALL MATTER AND ENERGY ROTATES WITH A GRADUAL DECREASE IN ROTATION AS THE DISTANCE FROM THAT BLACK HOLE INCREASES SUCH THAT THE MOMENT OF ROTATION CANNOT BE MEASURED BY ANYTHING EXCEPT GRAVITY WAVE PERTURBATIONS AS DOES IN THE LIGO PROJECT WHICH WILL MEASURE SPACE -TIME CURVATURE AT GREAT DISTANCES. Naturally, according to the math

$i\,(n)$abcd $\equiv \Pi(n = 1$ to $\infty)$ eigenstates of $2^n + 1\pi\omega$ i $\rightarrow j\ 2^{n\pi\omega}\ j$ $\rightarrow$ i $+ 2\pi/R$ abc $+$ or $-\frac{1}{2}$r g$\frac{ab}{+}$ or $-$ ihΛ ba$(\rho$ ab$)$ compactifies to a circle or C = 0 + 2πR where the circumference is curved Riemannian or Lorenzian Space = time over an infinite number of eigenstates whose infinte product become $0\frac{or\,1}{\infty}$ + 2π(*Riemann forces of nature*) *and the circle was described above with + or – i is* Wick *Rotated among dimensions describing time as ict as the fourth dimension acting on the wave function from the Schrodinger Equation as* - iℏ(*Ψ)* of the point particle r, t and describes the energy density of everything as the cosmologic c

Constant of b on a times the energy density of matter of a acting on b. The Cosmologic Constant is the energy density of a vacuum (curves space-time outward) with only the mass of the background microwave radiation while rho ab (curves space-time inward) forms the composite energy density of everything formed from the Ricci Tensor suggesting inertial mass R ab(ℏ) = ρ ab.

MATHEMATICAL PROOF OF THE FIRST EVENT BEING THE TIME OSCILLATION PARADOX OF THE INFINITE PARALLEL PLANES

According to the Gupta-Bleuler Quantization the tachyon exists at the 0 energy eigenstate relating to D-0-Branes. Tachyon → |0 > *where the massless vector is a* 1 ‡|0 > *and the massless scalar is* $k\mu a1$ $^{\ddagger}\mu$|0 > *and massless spin 2 vector boson in fermionic or vacuum state is a1#(mu)a1#(nu)|0> with massive vector a2#(mu)|o>*

11

CHAPTER THREE

TACHYONS AND FERMIONS WITH REGARD TO THE FIRST EVENT; EVERYTHING IS SOMETHING AND NOTHING DOESN'T EXIST

The products of all Fock Spaces for all Harmonic Oscillators... ∇ n ... q in the tensor virial theorem for the Ontologic Proof of God) *(infinite number) yields an eigen-state Пn, µ{a n‡,µ}/0 >* whereby the harmonic oscillators yields the ground state or eigenstate $= 0 \dfrac{or \Pi (n=0)1}{2^n} + 1\pi\varpi i \rightarrow \dfrac{j}{2^{2\pi\omega j}} \rightarrow$ ior the infinite number of D – 0 – Branes or the infinite parallel planes. The spectrum of the lowest lying eigenstates have tachy (infinite parallel planes with infinitely dilated time). Tachyons existed in the lowest eigen-state or the ground state (zero dimensional state) and were an integral part of the space continuum existing at v>c while fermions (the fermionic vacuum state)were at v<c where c=3x10^8 meters/sec. Each and every Fock Space is composed of the energy equivalent of hadrons which are massless as space is massless. The Fermions which are massless comprise of leptons for the fabric of space or the sum total of all Fock Space (down to and even below the Hilbert Space limit which relates with Planck Length (10^-33cm). The quantum dot principle described in this author's first book "Mega-physics: A New Look at the Universe

"subdivided below the Hilbert Space limit and as the components of Hilbert and Fock Space is comprised of leptons which are 99.999% potential energy being held in the fabric of space by massless gluons as it's energy equivalent. Of course the ground state energy levels of leptons and gluons as miniscule as they are both virtually massless as also indicating the initial vacuum state prior to the First Event.

Regee Trajectories for open strings illustrate that the tachyon is the God Particle prior to the formation of the spin 2 vector boson after the first event (time oscillation) which formed the Higgs Field. Fock Space for each any every Harmonic Oscillator (;see tensor virial theorem in the Vortex Model Ontologic Proof). The Fermionic Vertex limit with very small Fock Space(s) is Q BRST|R>=0 with an infinite number of Fermionic verticies. The infinite number of Fermionic verticies→ *utilize the same onshell matrix element. Φ is the vanishing anticommutation relation and BRST*

IS THE CHARGE. V=[Q BRST, *Φ] WHERE Q is nilpotent. There are an infinite number of vertex functions in vacuua*

And each vertex function represents a plane of space without time where all planes are totally parallel with a Regge Slope of 0. Theses vacuaa are e^qϕ(0)|0 ≥ |q > *and the conformal weight is* $\frac{1}{2}$ $\varepsilon q(q + Q)$ *where the fermionic and vertex finctions are each infinity corresponding to the infinite nu* ber *of parallel planes before* the time oscillation paradox between fermions and tachyons which both were part of a continuum forming the spin 2 vector bosons in the vortex of space-time caused by the oscillation of time causing the spin and centrifuge effect forming the string dimensions. V 3/2=[Q BRSTε V 1/2] ... V 5/2[Q BRST, ε V 3/2] ... ad infinitum. All these verticies are equivalent to each other AND TH THEY ARE INFINIT

FERMIONIC -FERMIONIC SCATTERING AMPLITUDES USING FORMALISM NET MIRROR IMAGE EFFECTS NETTING ZERO. AS THE FERMIONIC STATE IS THE VACUUM STATE WITH AN INFINITE NUMBER OF PLANES ARE NO DIMENSIONS THE FERMIONIC VERTICIES ALL NET THE FUEL FOR EVERYTHING WITH THE TACHYON BEING THE POTENTIATOR WHEN A ROGUE TACHYON DROPS TO THE SPEED OF LIGHT CAUSING THE TIME OSCILLATION BETWEEN TIME's ARROW GOING FORWARD AND BACKWARD.

BASED ON THESE CONCLUSIONS SPACE ITSELF IS COMPRISED OF FERMIONS AND TACHYONS. UNDER THE SPEED OF LIGHT FERMIONS ARE THE AETHER OR QUINTESSANCE AND THE INFINITE NUMBER OF PARALLEL PLANES ARE COMPRISED OF FERMIONS UNDER THE SPEED OF LIGHT AND TACHYONS ABOVE THE SPEED OF LIGHT. It's like a totally blank blackboard with no contents or points (intersection of three planes). The blackboard in this case is comprised of fermions and tachyons with the speed of light boundary being a dichotomy or boundary or interface between tachyons and fermions where the sum total of fermions and tachyons equals the dimension of time once the speed of light boundary was breeched by either fermions or tachyons. Space under the speed of light is comprised of fermions and above the speed of light comprised of tachyons and at the speed of light space-time constricts toward zero as mentioned in my books "Mega-physics II; An Explanation of Nature" and "The Equation of Everything". So prior to the first event there we no points as there were no plane intersections and the intersection of three planes form a point. The planes were composed of fermions and tachyons; depending on the velocity and time's arrow (Tachyons backwards; Fermions time forwards) Space=fermions (tachyons) and are dependent on velocity which form the dimension of time when the fermions and tachyons are mixed. When this occurs the spin 2 vector bosons are formed with mass, the Higgs Field, and time wraps around space constricting or dilating it. Space

() no dimensions=velocity of fermions with respect to the speed of light+ or -velocity of tachyons with respect to the speed of light. {} = $\frac{d(0)\,fermions}{dt}$ + or − d(0)tachyons/dt and c=0 space-time. So c=d(fermions/dt)+ or - d(tachyons)/dt. So as fermions and tachyons comprise space and are the components of space and as the intersections of these special planes are zero in the zero dimensional state; the fermionic space and tachyonic space were separated by the boundary of the speed of light which has zero space-time. As the fermionic state is the vacuum state and space is comprised of fermions the fermions are leptons and gluons where leptons and gluons are massless as the previous book "What is the Dimension of Time?" proved that space-time is massless, then before the first event the derivative of the sum total of fermions with respect to time=0infinitely dilated) and the derivative of the sum total of tachyons with respect to time=0 (infinitely dilated) also equals 0. (note quarks and anti-quarks have a variable mass but quarks and anti-quarks didn't form from gluons until after the Oscillating Time Paradox). Based on the concept that the advent of the time oscillation or paradox occurred at exactly 3x10^8 meters/sec or the speed of light; THIS POINT IS WHERE TIME BEGAN AND WHERE TIME BEGAN CONSTRICTING AND DILATING SPACE. From the Lorenzian Transformation time dilates toward infinity at the speed of light or in essence stops as space-time constricts toward zero at this point. IN THAT MATTER OF SPEAKING TIME'S ORIGIN WAS AT THE SPEED OF LIGHT AS THAT IS WHERE SEQUENCING OF EVENTS STARTED AND IN A SENSE THE SPEED OF LIGHT BOUNDARY COULD BE CONSIDERED TIME WITH SPACE EIXSTING ABOVE AND BELOW THIS BOUNDARY. ALSO AS THE SPEED OF LIGHT IS A CONSTANT NOT A VARIABLE TIME CAN BE ELIMINATED TOTALLY FROM THE EXPRESSION ds/dt as dt→ ∞ and s → ∞ as space − time constricts toward 0 making distance → ∞. THIS IS SYNONYMOUS WITH THE WORM HOLE PHENOMENON. *Note* the Harmonic Oscillator in the tensor virial theorem is ∇x and Γ is the spherical index boundary. ∇x reveals the infinite harmonic oscillators involved

In the Fermionic vertex model and tachyon model revealing the 0 eigen-state or ground state.

Hadrons are composed of bosons and fermions where the Higgs Boson is massive and subcomponents of fermions comprise leptons and the six flavors of quarks (which have mass while gluons are massless)

PRIOR TO THE FIRST EVENT LEPTONS AND GLUONS WERE AN INTEGRAL PART OF SPACE. AFTER THE FIRST EVENT QUARKS, GLUONS AND LEPTONS WERE INVOLVED WITH SPACE AFTER THE TIME OSCILLATION WHICH FORMED THE VORTEX OF SPACE-TIME WITH THE STRING DIMENSIONS. SPIN 2 VECTOR BOSONS ALSO FORMED AFTER TIME CONSTRICTED AND DILATED SPACE. TACHYONS INCORPORATE WITH THE HIGGS BOSON IN THE 'GOD PARTICLE' AFTER THE FIRST EVENT AND EXISTED WITHOUT THE HIGGS FIELD BEFORE THE FIRST EVENT.

Quarks are composed of strings as they have mass. Strings also have mass so the next question is did strings always exist or have their inception only after the first event? Spin 2 vector bosons only existed after the first event which described gravity which is the curvature of space-time caused by mass. Mass must exist as a pre-requisite for gravity to exist. Therefore as quarks have mass, they curve space-time which means it must be a post-requisite of the first event. As strings have mass albeit negligible; they must post-requisite the first event; as are photons which have a negligible mass which isn't zero. Also the formation of the string dimensions must form at the same time as strings. However space must be composed of something that pre-requisites strings without it being nothing but must have zero gravity. This therefore can't be quarks, mesons or even neutrinos; although baryons may qualify. Despite this GLUONS FORM QUARKS AND ENCOMPASS A SUPERSTRONG FORCE AND THE FRACTURE OF GLUONS CAN INVOLVE A SINGULARITY LIKE A BIG CRUNCH OR BIG RIP WITH ENORMOUS FORCE FAR GREATER THAN THE STRONG FORCE. GLUONS ARE MASSLESS AS ARE LEPTONS AND THE GLUONS MAY HOLD SPACE-TIME TOGETHER WHILE THE LEPTONS ARE THE PARITITONS OF SPACE-TIME WHICH ARE BEING HELD TOGETHER. THE FABRIC OF FLUID SPACE IS COMPRISED OF LEPTONS AND GLUONS HOLD SPACE TOGETHER. AS THE LAW OF CONSERVATION OF ENERGY STATES THAT ENERGY CAN NEITHER BE CREATED NOR DESTROYED THE COMPONENTS OF SPACE SUCH AS GLUONS, LEPTONS AND TACHYONS MUST BE COMPRISED OF ENERGY AS THEY ARE MASSLESS. ENERGY ALWAYS EXISTED AND ALWAYS WILL EXIST. THE GLUONS AND LEPTONS WERE INITIALLY 100% POTENTIAL ENERGY HOLDING TOGETHER THE FABRIC OF SPACE AND COMPRISING THE FABRIC OF SPACE UNTIL THE FABRIC OF SPACE WAS DISRUPTED AND TRANSFORMED BY THE TIME PARADOX CAUSED BY A ROGUE TACHYON TRAVELING AT V=C WHERE THE PARADOX OCCURRED.

The distance between each and every manifold in the infinite plane hypothesis approaches zero without reaching it as it is the zero dimensional state. Basically, the static energy of the components of space comprised of leptons and gluons acts as a "cushion" between the planes or manifolds to prevent the manifolds from touching each other (.See diagram 1). It also keeps the manifolds intact.

$R\infty$ $(a, 0,0,0)$ = the Region in Topological space whereby the potential energy of gluons holding the fabric of Space together is "a" being acted upon by b,c,d where b,c, and d are the tensors which are zero (0). R a refers to the potential energy of the sumtotal of all the manifolds or planes which are cushioned by the potential energy of each and every other plane or manifold. Therefore R(a,0,0,0)=-R(a,0,0,0) and the region of topological space of R+(-R)→ 0. *If the sum was zero it would define dimensions yet it must be zero as the scintilla between* each manifold would be space-less-ness and as energy always existed and requires space to exist; this option isn't possible; therefore the partition between each manifold must be a membrane which adheres to each manifold or surface by the potential energy of the gluons. So as a result D-0-branes=R(a,0,0,0) where a is the gluon potential energy adhering the manifold to the D-0-brane and preventing the manifolds from being in contact with each other which is a requirement for being perfectly parallel and therefore the zero dimensional state.

Note there may be a negligible repulsive force between the energies of leptons and gluons acting as the cushion;however this would only occur if there was a flattening effect of space as time was infinitely dilated resulting in anti-gravity as suggested by the Cosmologic Constant or 10^-53 or the energy density of a vacuum or the vacuum state rather than the false vacuum of deep space therefore there must be a repulsive force suggestive of anti-gravity even in the absence of any measurable mass from leptons or gluons. *R∞ a, 0,0,0 or the Region of Space = Λ a + Σ D − 0 − BRANES whereby the potential energy of the D − 0 − Branes = potential energy of leptons + potential energy of gluons → 10!!joules as mentioned in this author!s previous book* What is the Dimension of Time. The cushion between each and every parallel plane or manifold is caused by the composite of the D-0-Brane composed of the potential energy of the gluons and leptons and the anti-gravity effect of the Cosmologic Constant. *Totalρ = ρ vacuum + ρ leptons + gluons. ρ vacuum = Λ and ρ leptons + gluons = 10!!joules as 100% potential energy which converted to kinetic energy after the time* Paradox which formed the space-time vortex and string dimensions. If the leptons and gluons were 100% kinetic energy it would either be contained in the infinite parallel planes or would leech into the region of topologic space between the infinite parallel planes. Considering all the possibilities there is sufficient kinetic energy to leech into the area between the parallel planes which are repelled by the antigravity space flattening effect of the Cosmologic Constant. As this area approaches zero without it being zero this kinetic energy component would be very small call it $\in K.\,E. \rightarrow 0$ *which separates each and every* $D - 0 - Branes.$ Mathematically therefore Λ *and* ρ *leptons* + *gluons* $= 10!!" + \rho\ 99.9999 - \epsilon\ P.\,E.\ for\ leptons\ and\ gluons)$ $+ \rho\ \epsilon\ K.\,E.\ for\ leptons\ and\ gluons.$ Remember that the Law of Conservation of Energy states that energy cannot be created or destroyed making energy a continuum(without beginning or ending) and as infinitely dilated time still exists as time and time always existed time is part of the space-time continuum. As a consequence time and energy always existed as well as space and they will always exist.

Utilizing E=mc^2 as an approximation ;at isn't exact ..... if E=10^77 joules and c^2=3x10^8 m/sec)^2 then the mass=10^77/9x10^16=1.1x10^93 kg of mass in all the universes in the space-time continuum. As a consequence of this as the mass of this universe is 10^64Kg then 10^29kg is spread out through the rest of the spacetime continuum. Despite this, there is empirical evidence of approximately 10^54kg as the mass of this universe leaving 1.1x10^103 kg mass in the space-time continuum. As 10^103 kg is inclusive of dark matter based on space-time curvature the other 10^29 kg is the forward momentum of space-time being acted upon by the momentum of other universes in the multi-verse. Again as the correction factor for hadrons and photons is m^2c^4+mc^2 then the mass becomes 10^77/c^6=10^77/3x10^48=1.3X10^125 kg.)^1/2 which is over a googlplex of mass as the components of mass of composed of hadrons. Because of this there are approximately 1.22x10^125kg)^1/2 in our universe/10^54kg in our universe universes based on mass. The number of universes in the multiverse was discussed as universes in the space-time continuum based on the correction factor of Einstein's equation as applied to massless or near massless hadrons traveling at or near the speed of light. Despite this, the mass of our universe is the square root of $1.3x10^{125}$ kg or $1.1x10^{63}$Kg which has extreme precision from the known value of 10^{54} kg utilized in this author's book "Mega-physics II: An Explanation of Nature" and "What is the Dimension of Time?" Physicists at Stanford University Andre Lindy and Vitalie Valchurin mentioned the extreme possibility that there are $10^{10^{16}}$ and maybe the possibility of $10^{10^{10^7}}$ or e ^{10} e$^{10^{10^7}}$ which are far greater than a googolplex. Based on calculations however, there may be 10^{10} universes in the multi-verse based on differential mass calculations. On other interesting point relates to the radius of this universe as being approximately 10^{10} light-years. Does this mean that the 10^{10} universes in the multi-verse have an average radius of 1 light-year;it seems more likely that the velocity of light changes throughout different formations of space-time curvature between the universes of the multi-verse twisting and turning based on the varied masses and being bent as gravity(curvature of space-time caused by mass)making it appear as though the mean radius of other universes is one light year when in reality the mass density of these disparate universes is greater and at times far greater than than our own which is primarily a near vacuum state. As an example;in older universes there may be a good deal more black holes than in our universe and this would skew the reading of space-time into a more spiral configuration making the radius and diameter(Schwarzchild) appear smaller than it actually is. This is more evidence of Obler's Paradox as proposed by Edgar Alan Poe who said that our universe is very young as the night sky is mostly dark rather than full of starsIt also implies that the Second Event was not necessarily the simultaneous formation of all the universes but had s sequential order in which our universe was later in the sequence. As a result the relative position of our universe in the space-time continuum while still close to the center of the vortex which is pulling us toward it at an accelerated rate may have other universes closer to the center of this huge space-time vortex formed from the First Event. Much of this will be discussed later.. This does not totally rule out the possibility of the existence of one universe however provides soft conclusive evidence that 10^64 kg reveals the total mass of all universes as space-time is relatively massless indicating that the frequency of black holes may either diminish or evaporate at a greater rate in other universes and that the formation of stars and galaxies may be in an earlier stage in some other local universes. It also indicates that a Big Crunch indicated in the book "What is the Dimension of Time?" accelerating the expansion geometrically by pulling the galaxies with a velocity of 2.2x10^35(c)meters/sec with the push of Dark Energy if forcing homogeneity and RELATIVE ISOTROPISM RATHER THAN ABSOLUTE ISOTROPISM with reference to the observer such as the WOMP or Hubble Space Telescope and that the Big Crunch is pulling the mass apart on a string level to fill the void of accelerating space-time in a diffusion like process as space-time is a perfect fluid. This means the mass is like a particle in a suspension in motion and as space-time increases in velocity homogeneity will increase, black hole evaporation may increase and the discernable edge will blur out more and more. This will make it possibly more difficult to determine the supermassive black holes including the site of "The Big Bang" unless space-time curvature measures are used as in the LIGO PROJECT. THE HAWKING PARADOX ABOUT INFORMATION BEING LOST IN AN EVAPORATING BLACK OUT IS ANSWERED AS THE DIFFUSION OF THE INFORMATION AT THE EVENT HORIZON OF BLACK HOLES INTO FLUID LIKE SPACE-TIME IS LIKE THE DISSOLUTION OF COFFEE INTO WATER. THE INFORMATION BECOMES A UNIFORM SUSPENSION IN FLUID SPACE-TIME AS WITH HAWKING RADIATION AND DIFFUSES OUT IN ALL DIRECTIONS AROUND THE POINT OF ORIGIN OF THE

DIFFUSION WHICH IS THE EVENT HORIZON AND THE SPUMING OUTWARD OF THE QUASAR. THIS MEANS THE INFORMATION FROM EACH AND EVERY EVAPORATING BLACK HOLE IS SMEARED THROUGHOUT SPACE WITH THE CONCENTRATION OF THE SMEAR DECREASING GEOMETRICALLY FROM THE POINT OF ORIGIN OF THE SMEAR ;information is preserved only extraordinarily difficult to detect. This is due to the "traffic jam" effect of matter existing in dilated time relative to the observer at the event horizon however over several hundred thousand years the information will "bleed through" enough to harmoniously diffuse out into space-time from the point off maximum constriction at the event horizon(Schwarzchild Space-time)to space which appears to be more and more asymptotically flat as the effect of the flattening of the Cosmologic Constant takes over.

CHAPTER FOUR: THE HARMONIC OSCILLATOR AND THE TIME PARADOX

CHAPTER FOUR

RIGOROUS PROOF THE HARMONIC OSCILLATOR AND THE TIME PARADOX

The Time Paradox of the First Event as a Harmonic Oscillator form strings and vibrations of space constricted and dilated by time as it oscillates, The Gupta-Bleurlen Quantization with Virosoro Constraints for the first event. Here $<\phi[L\ f]\psi > 0$. The action S of a 2x2 matrix of g ab = δ ab$_0^{-1}$ $_{-1}^{\ 0}$ reveals the free string and equations of motion with Conformal Gauge Symmetry parameterization and Weyl's Conformal Tensor suggesting Weyl's Invariance. $S = \dfrac{1}{4\pi\alpha \int_0^\pi d\sigma \int d\tau(x * \mu^2 - x\mu^2)}$

$\neq 0$ whereby σ is space τ is time x $^{*2\mu}$ have μ as the relative velociy = ties *of the equations of motion of the free uncoupled string. The limits of integration for τ oscillate between infinity and zero and zero and infinity depending on whether time's arrow points forward or backward in the oscillation.1* α relates to the period of oscillation acted upon space by time. So the action S

$= \dfrac{1}{4\pi\alpha \int_0^\pi d\sigma \int_\pi^0 d\tau \int_0^\pi d\tau\ whereby\ d\tau\ (x'\mu^2}$ $- $ xμ^2 reverse accirding

to the oscillation of time. A flat plane σ is described by π radians and tim??? oscillates along 2 pi radians or the circumference of a circle. Again S=1/4$\pi\alpha \int_0^\pi d\sigma \int_\pi^0 d\tau \int_\pi^0 d\tau$ and $(d\tau(x'\mu^2 - x\mu^2)$

reverse according to the oscillation of time. The compactification of this universe is a circle C=2πR where C – circumference is space – time formed initally as a Harmonic Oscillator. Space – time = $\frac{space}{mass}$ and space was a constant prior to the oscillation of time where time is the Harmonic Osciator. Space was initially a constant(k) and the mass was approximately zero as space was almost massless prior to the time oscillation paradox. This meant that space-time=space which was infinity=was ∞. $\frac{k}{\delta}$ and *this goes with the infinite planes of space in dilated time. Time was dilated to ∞ so sp time was also ∞. ε = very small number as space isn't totally massless due to negligible mass of leptons and gluons*

ε∞ = ∞ so space – time and space were both infinite and k = ∞.

The partial second derivative with regard to space and time with regard to x at velocity **M(Σ, T)** = *0 where σ =* space and τ is time equal zero. Note boundaries x' μ *(0. τ)* = 0 and x' μ *(π, τ)* = 0 as 0 and π are the limits of integration of totally flat planes σ. $x^{\mu(\sigma,\tau)}$ = x $1^{\mu(\sigma+\tau)}$+ x2$^{\mu(\sigma-\tau)are}$ the solutions to the boundaries. The canonnical commutation [Pu(σ), xυ(σ')] = iηηνδ(σ – σ') where δ(σ, σ') = 1/π(1 + 2$\sum_1^\infty$ cos nισ *cos* nσ' where n = *0* is the preoscilllation phase before the first event. With the canonical commutations the harm

Harmonic oscillator of the commutation
[aημ, a^ * mυ] = δ mn ηημν and the oscillators are α m^μ = m)^1/2 a m^μ *and* α – m^μ = (m)^1/2 a * m^μ *both of which have m(mass)>0. This is based on n eigen-states. H=*$\int_0^\pi d\sigma$ *(Pμx' μ – L)* = πα' $\int$ + 1/2 α'π)^2 X'^2 μ)dσ = $\sum_1^\infty$ na * nμaη$^\mu$ + pμ$^{2(\alpha')\alpha}$ 0μ = $\sqrt{2\alpha'\ p\mu}$. This makes an infinite shift in the zero point energy with the mass of the lowes??? order particle which is not well defined but is the tachyon again proving it always existed was never created and couldn't be destroyed. The Hamiltonian diagonal operator acting upon Fock Space with the Harmonic Oscillator of time causes each oscillation mode to be uncoupled from

the other oscillation modes. According to Regee Trajectories; the massless spin 1 particle (tachyon, lepton and gluon) is the maximum on a Yang Mills Field with an Infinite number of Regee

Trajectories $\int_{\epsilon}^{\infty} d\tau \int_{\infty}^{\epsilon} d\tau \int_{\delta}^{\pi} d\sigma \int_{\pi}^{\delta} d\sigma$ yielding an infinite number of excitations or eigen-states for the Relativistic String.

The tachyon triggers the Harmonic Oscillator to form the string dimensions in previously static space. Again the 0 dimensional eigen-state is described by $\Pi_{\eta\mu}\{a\eta, \mu\}|0 >$. *The static space is in infinite volume* $S =$ h$\left(\dfrac{1}{4\pi\psi}\right) \int d\tau \int_{\delta}^{\infty} d\sigma \rightarrow 2\pi R$ *with limits of time* $\tau(\tau)$ *being beng ϵ to ¥. The action $S = \hbar(¥)1/\pi(1 + 2\Sigma_{i}^{i}$ cos nσ cos nσ' as space σ is dilated and constricted by the harmonic oscillator of infinitely*

Note

$h = h\dfrac{}{2\pi}$ and $h\dfrac{}{2\pi} = \dfrac{1}{4\pi\alpha}$ so $h = \dfrac{1}{2\alpha}$ so α = the sum total of all Riemann Force of Nature at the time of the first event or α = $\dfrac{1}{2}\left(\dfrac{1}{h}\right)$ *It should be noted that the physical laws that dictate matter and energy are limited to the system in which the first event is measured. It should be noted that* $\mu = 2r = \dfrac{r}{h}$ *where μ= free energy* r = Riemann forces 2r = total Riemann forces + or – and h = Planck's Constanet. This results in $\mu = 10^{77}$ joules. *Mass follows the equations of mass, energy follows the equations of energy, gravity is the curvature of space-time caused by mass, momentum is mass times velocity etc. Space can be contorted and twisted by time but cannot be broken, created or destroyed. If there is a multi-verse are the same laws of physics for mass and energy be the same as our universe? The laws of space and space-time must be the same as string theory states that time is the same in all universes but the laws that govern space must also be the same. Despite this the laws of motion, acceleration, displacement and how much space-time is contorted or changed by mass may be different. On cannot assume that if the total mass of our universe is 10^64kg and the total mass of the multi-verse is 1.22x10^63kg or approximately 10^64 kg that* *this proves conclusively that there is only one universe. Mass may be totally different in other universes; and although -mass is almost a non-sequitor it may be possible as strange mass, oscillating mass (mass/i) or the lack of sensitivity of our recording and measuring devices. Also the observer must be considered and the sensitivity of the observer as well as what's to be observed. Even measurements of space-time curvature isn't as sophisticated enough to determine many characteristics of other universe (the measuring device is part of what's being measured), Example: does anti-matter have the same or different effects on space-time curvature or gravity as strange matter or matter? Despite this the first event which formed the string dimensions, matter must be the seed for the multi-verse assuming that other universes follow M theory. Please note that by the S or action in infinitely dilated time equals infinity this conclusively proves that the Regee Trajectories dropped from v>c to v=c initiating the time paradox and oscillation as the INITIAL EVENT ACTING UPON THE INFINITE PARALLEL PLANES. V>c are the tachyons traveling at greater than $3x10^{\wedge}8m/sec$ and v=c are the tachyons traveling at $3x10^{\wedge}8m/sec$. Note that $1/2\pi h = (6.63x10^{34})$ joule – sec $\left(\frac{14}{22}\right)$ or 1/3 which is $2.21x10^{\wedge}34$ joule-sec which is the sum total of all Riemann Forces of Nature at the first event. The pi's cancel making the equation $\mu = 2r = 10^{77}$ joules which is the total free energy whereby r is the positive Riemann Forces or nature*

CHAPTER 4.2

WAS THE QUANTUM BUBBLE THE FIRST MATTER/ANTI-MATTER FORMED AFTER THE FORMATION OF STRING DIMENSIONS?

This is debatable. If it's true that the is only one universe, the answer is YES. Also, a multiverse and a single universe can form from the first event. The quantum bubble was formed from the Infinite Parallel planes hypothesis and space always existed with time (infinitely dilated) so time always existed as well. If everything was in the quantum bubble this makes no sense as nothing doesn't exist and the Quantum Bubble was 10^24 cm and there has to be something outside the quantum bubble; so as a conclusion the quantum bubble doesn't contain everything. The formation of matter with mass formed the spin 2 vector boson which described the effect of gravity. With mass, gravity and the string dimensions you can have the quantum bubble formed with the multiverse or just our universe. Also the quantum bubble may have been one of a near infinite number of quantum bubbles (10^10^10^7) QUANTUM BUBBLES OR e10e10e7. This is 7 times a googolplex of quantum bubbles forming 7 times a googolplex of universes. Now as a conclusion if the different mass calculations of 10^64kg for our universe and 1.22x10^63 kg in the multiverse this implies but doesn't prove that there is only one universe. Also one must consider that the laws of physics may be slightly or radically different in other universes and that matter may be strange, hybrid, or oscillating in other universes. So as a result this author is agnostic on this point. It doesn't matter because there was a Big Bang for our universe and it does have a center of mass at the site of the Big Bang;so far out that measuring devices even with space-time curvature measurements or gravity waves it would take possibly half a million to a billion years to locate the curvature reflecting the rotational vectors of space-time as the site of the Big Bang. As a result one must use other means to show a multiverse like the dark flow measurements or CMB data at USC's Planck Team. The universe doesn't contain everything and does have an interface(if spherical the edge is rounded in to a sphere with a circumference of $2\pi R$) *is also the compactification of string theory or M Theory but even this* doesn't prove one universe as string theory may not be the rules of other universes. Despite this there is evidence that this is the only universe and the evidence of a multiverse; while there, is not as much as that of the one universe. There is also the possibility that the quantum bubble always existed ;however that leaves questions like, if matter always existed how did the matter form? If there was mass where did the mass come from? As a result the formation of the quantum bubble or the googolplex of quantum bubble were the result of the 4.3 SECOND EVENT. WHY AREN'T PHOTONS THE MASSLESS COMPONENTS OF SPACE? Photons travel at v=c by definition and are almost massless 3×10^{-18} eV/c^2. The fermionic state is the vacuum state according to Physicists such as Michio Kaku and Dr. Roger Penrose and fermions are made of leptons(which are massless) and gluons(which are massless) which comprise Quarks which have mass. So why isn't space(before the time oscillation paradox)comprised of photons or photons and gluons?If space was comprised of photons then the infinite parallel planes would be at v=c before the paradox and when the rogue tachyon dropped to v=c that would trigger the paradox. Photons have mass albeit negligible and so do leptons and gluons therefore space has negligible mass. If photons have a negligible mass at the speed of light (in which photons travel)the mass should increase according to the Lorenzian Transformation mass=mass $0/1-V^2/c^2=\infty$ *but of course veolcity* = !!!"!!!"# − ϵ. It is possibly that the pure energy which is almost 100%potential energy and a scintilla of kinetic energy to separate the planes along with the Cosmologic Constant has the kinetic energy IN THE FORM OF PHOTONS and the potential energy in the form of LEPTONS AND GLUONS. Note also that photons according to our present knowledge are very very old and may have existed at the time of the first event. If this is true photons mixed with the rogue tachyon at the speed of light to initiate the time oscillation paradox whereby the photons moved time forward and the rogue tachyon moved time backwards cohabiting the same space.

4.4 CAN TACHYONS CONVERT ENERGY INTO MATTER?

IF THE TACHYON WITH THE SUBSEQUENT HIGGS FIELD AND MASSIVE HIGGS BOSON ARE THE GOD PARTICLE(S)AND IF THE HIGGS FIELD CONVERTS ENERGY INTO MATTER;THEN TACHYONS CAN CONVERT ENERGY INTO MATTER WITH THE FORMATION OF THE FIRST SPIN 2 VECTOR BOSON FROM THE ROGUE TACHYON THAT DROPPED TO THE SPEED OF LIGHT FROM GREATER THAN THE SPEED OF LIGHT.

CHAPTER FIVE

WHAT CAME FIRST; THE BIG BANG OR THE FORMATION OF THE MULTI-VERSE?

The Big Bang was preceded by a quantum bubble of approximately 50% matter and 50% anti-matter. How did this precise mix form? The most plausible explanation was a collision of two membranes which comprised of a matter universe with physical laws consistent with matter and an anti-matter universe with laws consistent with anti-matter. Of course when anti-matter and matter collide they form an explosion annihilating a goodly percentage of each but there was an IMPLOSION or a BIG CRUNCH with the commixing or collision of the two membranes associated with the two universes. The Big Crunch resulted when the impact of two universes which distorted or disrupted space-time to the degree that it caused a Big Crunch. There is also the possibility of a three way collision between a matter universe, anti-matter universe and a vacuum universe consisting of only space and energy. In the 700×10^{10} googlplex of universes postulated at Stanford University the likelihood of vacuum universes is high ; and they would force the matter and anti-matter universes INTO the vacuum universe to fill the vacuum and it's related space crunching space-time down to 10^{-24} cm in a mix or anti-matter and matter. This of course rotated and the matter settled at one pole and the antimatter at the opposite pole with the 0,0 point in the center whereby a symmetrical throat was formed and was the site of the Big Bang at 10^-43 seconds later(Planck Time).

Of course if it wasn't for the 50:_50 mix of anti-matter and matter one could have presumed that the quantum bubble was formed after matter and the string dimension were formed. Indeed, matter and anti-matter could have been formed then but NOT IN A 50:50 mix. Although with our present scientific knowledge we may be able to ascertain that the universe does have a center of mass at the site of the Big Bang by the increased rotational vectors of space-time as the region is approached by measuring gravity waves; determining if there was a three way collision of membranes developing into a Big Crunch or a two-way collision of membranes developing into a Big Crunch may be beyond our scientific expertise as the Big Bang ex nihilo(out of nothing) was acknowledged no matter how perverse it appears. Also the idea that this universe has no center of mass when Sir Isaac Newton stated that everything with mass has a center of mass or gravity ;and the universe has a mass of 10^64 kg .iso-tropism is relative based on the observer's relative position which decries the idea of Quantum Mechanics that when an observer is part of what's being observed the results are skewed by the limits of the system being observed. So basically, the universe may not have an edge but does have an interface with space-time comingling into space-time from other universes in the multi-verse. Space exists outside this universe as space-time and not nothing]. There is soft evidence that 10^10^10^10^7 universes exist in the multi-verse; if our universe had no center of mass or gravity it would be expanding in all directions from what]?Whether expanding from Inflation or a mutual repulsion of antiparticles and particle-anti-particle annihilation in the quantum bubble the 0,0 point which is the point of maximum rotation the rotation and expansion must be ASCERTAINABLE AND MEASURABLE IN ORDER FOR THE BIG BANG TO HOLD. Even the Steady-State

Theory has to begin with the Infinite Parallel Planes Hypothesis in which case the galaxies and universes formed when matter and anti-matter and all types of strange matter or hybrid matter form as the SECOND EVENT.

5.2 THE LAW OF CONSERVATION OF DIMENSIONS

THE LAW OF CONSERVATION OF DIMENSIONS in "Mega-physics, A New Look at the Universe" (2003) stated that the total number of a dimensions in a system must remain a constant. A system is defined as a set or subset which is bounded. In the case of the first event the infinite parallel planes comprised of potential energy from gluons, leptons, and tachyons composed one and only one system; the zero dimensional system. After the first event a new system or subsystem was formulated which comprised of matter, energy, and all the dimensions which intail string theory($26 \rightarrow \infty$). This results in a different system or subsystem to the zero dimensional state before the event even comprised of D-0-Branes. All the remaining membranes were formed after the first event as potential energy turned into matter and kinetic energy, heat, electromagnetism, the Strong Force, the weak force and either other universes or the quantum bubble were formed. Once this subsystem was formed it was non-Abelian as the components were necessary and although the components of space (gluons, leptons and tachyons) existed before and after the first event. This is because no planes are totally parallel after the first event as space-time was originally spiral and a vortex with string dimensions gravitating toward the center due to the effect of the spin 2 vector bosons. Therefore the total number of dimensions before the first event=0 and after the first event = 1 to ∞ *so the total number of dimensions of each system or subsystem were a constant although a again space cannot be created or destroyed. {0} before the first event regarding dimensions and {1,2,3,...26 ... ¥}after the first event. The comonents* pre and post first event include {tachyons, fermions} and after the first event were {tachyons, fermions {gluons, leptons}, spin 2 vector bosons, The Higgs Boson, quarks, neutrinos and all other inclusive hadrons are all composed of strings, potential energy, kinetic energy, heat, electromagnetism, the Strong Force, the Ultra-strong Force (released with the disruption of gluons in the fabric of space being held by leptons) and Orbifolds which are inclusive of Fock Space, Hilbert Space deSitter Space and anti-deSitter Space. Note that the null set {} is impossible, but {0} is the zero dimensional state containing an infinite number of parallel planes is possible, likely and did occur.

CHAPTER 5.3 HOW DID GRAVITY FORM?

Gravity is the curvature of space-time caused by mass. Before the first event space was infinite and mass was negligible caused by leptons, gluons and tachyons (plus possibly photons). During the first event the spin 2 vector boson was formed from the primordial tachyons and fermions during the time oscillation paradox. The rogue tachyon(s) dropped to the speed of light v=c and then was transformed into a massive Higgs Field ;which is spiral in configuration according to the Tensor Virial Theorem(see book "What is the Dimension of Time? ". This massive Higgs Field perturbed space-time into a spiral configuration during the time oscillation forming a spin and centrifuge effect. During the spin component the Higgs Boson underwent a clockwise and counterclockwise spin or (+ or – spin)for each component of the boson cohabiting the Higgs Field and the components of the spin 2 vector caused by the boson helped form the vortex of the Higgs Field and well as that of space-time form. Mathematically this author first book "Mega-physics, A New Look at the Universe" showed that

$$\int_{\epsilon}^{\infty} \frac{du}{u}$$

=lnu

→ln0=ϵ(approching zero but not 0 as ε was the kinetic energy that always existed

Space was composed of leptons and gluons which were almost 100% potential energy but a very small component was kinetic energy which prevented the infinite parallel planes of space from contacting each other as contact between two parallel planes would have produced a space paradox prior to the time paradox as since time is the sequencing of all events having an event such as a space paradox prior to the first event regarding time couldn't happen. If time is infinitely dilated before and after any event including a space paradox then a space paradox wouldn't be an event. As a space paradox is an event and requires time as a necessary component or pre-requisite of the paradox; a space paradox couldn't happen without time.

CHAPTER SIX

THE BIG BANG

AS DESCRIBED IN THIS AUTHOR'S PREVIOUS BOOK "MEGAPHYSICS II: AN EXPLANATION OF NATURE" THERE WAS A ROTATIONAL COMPONENT TO THE QUANTUM BUBBLE WHEREBY ANTI-MATTER ROTATED IN ONE DIRECTION AND MATTER ROTATED IN THE OPPOSITE DIRECTION WITH THE ROTATIONAL VECTORS GRAVITATING TO THE OPPOSING POLES AS IN A CENTRIFUGE WHICH WAS 10^{-24} cm. With the rotation of matter and anti-matter being 180 degrees from each other and gravitating toward the poles the fracture point with the symmetrical throat which resulted was what this author called the 0,0 point as per the first book "Mega-physics, A New Look at the Universe". As antiparticles express anti-gravity or repulsion to other anti-particles the mutually repulsive force gravitated to he center due to the extreme rotation in opposite directions of matter and anti-matter at the poles. The combination of the mutually repulsive force forming Dark Energy with its anti-gravity and the annihilation of most anti-matter with matter CAUSED THE BIG BANG(Mega-physics II: An Explanation of Nature)and resulted 6.75 x10^{34} erg during the first second of The Big Bang. This of course explained the paucity of anti-matter, the cause of the Big Bang and what Dark Energy is. Space-time was original spiral immediately after the first event; the Time Paradox oscillation but after the Big Bang there was a combination of rotation and expansion of space-time simultaneously with the rotational vector diminishing while the expansion vector was increasing. As a consequence any center of mass for this universe will show up with an increasing rotation in space-time curvature with gravity wave measurements as in the LIGO project (see What is the Dimension of Time?") This would approach the site of The Big Bang and the light of this supermassive black hole is such as distance from the Hubble Telescope 10^10 light years that as a black hole the equipment for detecting an absence of light may lack the sensitivity to detect it even if the light from that site has reached us and can be measured. Even at 10^5 light years which is 100,000 years for the light to reach the Hubble IT IS THE ABSENCE OF LIGHT AT THE EVENT HORIZON OF THE SUPERMASSIVE BLACK HOLE AT THE SITE OF THE BIG BANG THAT NEEDS TO BE MEASURED BUT CAN'T AS THAT LIGHT IS COMPLETELY ABSORBED INTO THE BLACK HOLE AND NOT REFLECTED. EVEN IF THE BLACK HOLE BECAME DRY OR INACTIVE AND DISSOLVED INRO SPACE LIKE A DIFFUSION OF SALT MIXING WITH WATER AS A SUSPENSION OF INFORMATION UNIFORMLY SPREAD THROUGHOUT SPACE, WITH OUR TECHNOLOGY THERE IS A LACK OF CAPACITY TO DETECT AND EVALUATE THIS SUSPENSION OF INFORMATION IN SPACE-TIME. This information would give vital evidence of the birth of this universe and while the WOMP in 1996 gave a general view of the universe with clumping of the Background Microwave Radiation after the Big Bang it's still incomplete, which is why the measurement of gravity waves showing space-time curvature is necessary to determine a double spiral configuration whereby one spiral or vortex is counterclockwise and the other clockwise illustrate the opposing rotations of matter and anti-matter before the orb blast. Of course as these vectors were 180 degrees from each other or π *radians the result was* π *radians clockwise and* π *radians counterclockwise as in the* Wick *Rotation of {x,y,z,ict} and {-x,-y,-z,-ic(-t)} or* $\pi - (-\pi)$ *radians where – reflects the opposite direction of the spin of antimatter to matter.* The C.P.T. Theorem (charge, parity, time) indicates that time and −time should be equivalent and with regard to Wick Rotation being heterotic (flipping between different dimensions) space-time which is negative only appears negative with respect to the x,y, and z axes not the -x,-y,-z axes so the resulting 2π *radians of the orb blast with a trajectory of π radians or* 180 *degrees holds.*

CHAPTER SEVEN

WHAT IS THE CONFIGURATION
OF THE MULTI-VERSE?

Space-time was originally a vortex after the first event and mathematically space-time curvature follows the spiral fractal formula according to Einstein in 1912 and this author's first book "Mega-physics, A New Look at the Universe" and the matter and anti-matter forming after the formation of strings and all Branes above the D-0-Brane progressed to form $10\wedge10\wedge10\wedge10\wedge7$ universes in the spiral space-time continuum with space-time diverging toward infinity in every and all directions except the center of the vortex. This is why space-time travels at $2.2x10\wedge35(c)$ meters. sec while in our universe it only travels at *πc acting as a current being pulled by space – time traveling at $2.2x10^{35(c)m}$ / sec.* The reason for the geometric acceleration of space-time is the push of Dark Energy and THE PULL OF SPACE-TIME FROM THE PERIPHERY TOWARDS THE CENTER OF THE VORTEX OF SPACE-TIME IN WHICH THE MULTIVERSE EXISTS. IT IS ALSO POSSIBLE THAT A BIG CRUNCH OCCURRED WHICH PULLED SPACE-TIME AT THAT VELOCITY TO FILL THE SUPERSTRONG FORCE OF THE DISRUPTION OF GLUONS ON LEPTONS IN SPACE-TIME. HOWEVER, IT IS MORE LIKELY ACCORDING TO OCCAM'S RAZOR that space-time is being pulled into the center of the space-time vortex. Recall Occam's Razor states that all things being equal the simplest explanation is generally the correct one and a singularity resulting in a Big Rip, tear or Crunch of space-time is less likely than space-time being pulled AS A PERFECT FLUID INTO THE CENTER OF THE SPACE-TIME VORTEX. The space-time continuum is spiral regardless of whether there is one universe or a multiverse of 700 googoplex or 10^{10^7} universes or more as the acceleration of space-time as a current radiates towards the center of the vortex and this acceleration is independent of the number of universes involved in the space-time continuum. Math based on the comparative mass of the universe and the multiverse implies one but that might be incomplete as again there is soft evidence of other universes. Acceleration is like a Big Flush of fluid like space-time with extraordinary angular momentum despite negligible mass due to the acceleration acting as a current in a perfect fluid region R(p). This is due to the velocity being $2.2x10^{35}(c)$ meters/sec.

7.2 WHERE IS OUR UNIVERSE'S RELATIVE POSITION IN THE SPACE-TIME CONTINUUM?

THE RELATIVE POSITION OF OUR UNIVERSE IN THE VORTEX IS BASED ON THE RATIO OF SPACE-TIME IN OUR UNIVERSE TO SPACE-TIME PULLING IT FROM THE REMAINDER OF THE SPACE-TIME CONTINUUM TO THE CENTER OF THE VORTEX. The velocity ratio is $\frac{\pi c}{2,2x10^{35}(c)}$ *which puts our universe in the region of space – time which has flatness equivalent to* $5x10^{-29}$ *radians or the total curvature of our universe.*

The flattening effect is from the Cosmologic Constant relating to Dark Energy and the enormous total pull of space-time onto space-time in our universe. The latter has a more powerful flattening effect than the weak force of Dark Energy. This relates to the mutual repulsion of anti-particles which is so sporadic in space due to great distances between each and every anti-particle that it makes the flatness of space-time primarily from space-times acceleration pull. As totally flat space-time is only possible when space is infinite and time infinitely dilated; totally flat space-time mimics the vacuum state of space with infinitely dilated time and is at the extreme outer periphery in all measurable and immeasurable directions. Despite this, still with an extreme velocity pulling on space-time (which is almost motionless) and the infinite space vacuum state or fermionic state is approached space-time curvature is best measure with our technology to determine the location of our universe in the space-time continuum.. Our universe while having extremely diminutive space-time curvature is relatively away from the center of the vortex but as $5x10^{-29}$ *is closer to 0 radians than 2π radians which is the center of the vortex of space – time which is doing the pulling on other space – time at the peripheries our universe is near the outer rim being close to a vacuum state over* most of the 10^10 light-years of space with galaxies occupying only a very small percentage of the space in our universe.

Are photons a continuum or not?

7.3 ARE PHOTONS A CONTINUUM OR NOT?

Photons are almost massless but they do have a miniscule mass although they do show gravitational effects such as at the event horizons of black holes; Light is bent by gravity and gravity is the curvature of space-time due to mass. Therefore light and other forms of electromagnetic radiation must have mass. This mass is the miniscule 3x10^-18 eV/c^2. Are photons composed of strings incorporating membranes such as the 1-Brane and 2-Brane which involved electric charge collection and distribution in space. These are described or expressed in conjunction with the 3-brane, 4-brane and distributed throughout higher levels of branes based on the dimensionality of space. Based on String and M theory photons are comprised of strings however with Relativistic Variance (Special Relativity states that photons travel at 3x10^8m/sec in a vacuum such as the false vacuum of deep space; however this conclusion doesn't incorporate Boso-Einsteinian Condensate or the temperature correction from the Background Microwave Radiation from The Big Bang which causes all thermometers (kelvin and centigrade to express temperatures which are 2.74 degrees colder tha they actually are.). In actuality photons are trapped in a matrix of Boso-Einsteinian Condensate at tem[eratures below 2.74 degrees kelvin and are stopped only vibrating in the matrix. Based on laser studies at near absolute zero photons (Dr. Lene Hau at Harvard) are decelerated from "c" toward 0 implying that photons are all electromagnetic radiation travels at all speeds except zero. Note the value of 3x10^-18 eV/c^2 is a non-resting mass for photons and a resting mass of 0 never occurs as photons still vibrate in the lattice of Boso-Einsteinian Condensate as a suspension. Therefore photons do have mass and are therefore composed of strings. Strings only formed after the First Event or the Time Oscillation Paradox so the statement. In the beginning there was darkness (the Infinite Parallel Planes or the Fermionic or vacuum state) and tachyons which comprised the pre-Higgs Boson and Field of the "God Particle" thus that statement appeard to be true albeit difficult to prove in th laboratory". Let there be light" incorporates electromagnetic radiation which only formed after the formation of strings after the First Event.

The converse view is that photons are totally massless and immortal which means they were incorporated into space with the Infinite Parallel Planes prior to the First Event. In that case photons would be a suspension in the space of the parallel planes trapped as a matrix similar to Boso-Einsteinian Condensate ar absolute zero (0 degrees kelvin) which was the temperature of the Infinite Parallel Planes rprior to the first event; however they may have also expressed the miniscule kinetic energy between the planes to kept the D-0 branes from being in contact with each other which would have formed dimensions. So was that kinetic energy from photons or leptons and gluons? As the release of the Super-strong Force occurred with the disruption of gluons in space during the First Event (potential energy transformed into kinetic energy) it would indicate that 100 percent potential energy isn't possible except at exactly absolute zero which can never be broached with the present forms of matter and our laws of physics although matter and strings weren't formed until after the First Event. (Odd forms of matter which were recorded at below absolute zero were really breeching 2.74 degrees kelvin and not absolute zero.) So the answer as to whether photons are "immortal" and part of the space continuum is still unclear unless and until the B.M.R. can be totally eliminated from the environment of the laboratories trying to breech absolute zero.

CHAPTER 7.4 A Mathematical Solution to the Mass Gap Problem in Yang Mills

Theory $1(I^{pc}) = \dfrac{3x10^{-18}ev}{c^2}$, $1(1--)$ for photons vibrating in a lattice structure as absolute zero is approached.

To Prove that for any compact simple gauge group G, a non-trivial quantum Yang-Mills theory exists in ¡ ^{4} *and has a mass gap* $\Delta > 0$. The Yang-Mills (non-Abelian) quantum field theory underlying the standard model of particle physics in ¡ ^{4} *euclidian space (flat space) has a mass gap* Δ *which is the mass of the least massive particle predicted in the theory.. The Mass gap is the* difference in energy between the vacuum and the next lowest energy state. The energy of a vacuum is 0 by definition and assuming that all energy states are particles in plane-waves with the mass gap being the mass of the lightest particle. For any given field $\phi(x)$ *the theory has a mass gap if the two point function has the property of* <$\phi(0, t)\phi(0,0) = \Sigma n\, A\, n\, e^\wedge - \Delta nt)$ *with* $\Delta o > 0$ being the eigenvalue for the lowest energy in the spectrum of the Hamiltonian and the mass gap. In lattice this mass gap occurs.

7.5 Photons and the Mass gap in a Lattice

Photons will vibrate in a lattice structure in Boso- Einsteinian Condensate at temperature just above absolute zero. This will add mass to the Boso -Einsteinian state regarding photons in the U(1) non-Abelian subgroup gauge symmetry group accounting for the mass gap. In terms of gauge symmetry with no resting frame the mass of a photon is $<10^{-18}$ electron volts/c2. The spin is 1, parity is - 1, charge (q)$<10^{-35}$ e and photons are stable during an indefinite period of time. The mass of a photon is such that the energy squared=momentum squared (c^2)+mass squared c^4 in other words $E^2=p^2c^2+m^2c^4$ where m→0. *Photons follow the CPT Theorem of charge, parity and time where reversal of time* doesn't affect the outcome.. Also the direction component of motion is $\pm\hbar$ *which is helical.* As there is no rest frame (photons vibrate as a Harmonic Oscillator) therefore there is no resting mass for photons although they are attracted or bent by gravity and therefore curve space-time as at the Event Horizon of a Black Hole. Utilizing the Harmonic Oscillator and applying this to the Ising Model in Conformal Field Theory will indicate the vibratory states of photons as the eigen-state of energy approaches 0 or the ground state as absolute zero is approached and the vibratory motion of photons is trapped in a lattice formation or MATHEMATICAL EXPOSITION; Boso-Einsteinian Condensate. Condensed; the gauge symmetry notation for intrinsic properties of photons would be 1(J^pc)=0,1(1--) where p=parity which is -1 and c is charge which is also -1. Spin is 1 and mass is listed as 0 in terms of gauge symmetry. Of course spin is translated into a Harmonic Oscillator and mass ≠ 0 *or is* $3x10^{-18}$ *eV/c^2*~0. In addition the C parity which is charge parity is also -1. So with a gauge symmetry of 1(J^pc)=0,1,(1--) and in the Mass gap equation the photon would be $<\Phi(0, t)\Phi(0,0)>$ *becomes* $< (0,1(1 - -)\Phi(0,0) > \rightarrow \Sigma$ *$Ane^{-\Delta nt}$ 1. In corporating this in to the Ising Model with regard to Conformal Field Theory* G/H=S U (2)k x SU(2)1/SU(2)k+1 where C G/H =3k/k+2+1-3(k+1)/(k+1)+2=1-6/(k+2)(k+3). Minimal unitary models exist such that m=k+2=3,4,5 and the unitary series is SU (2)k x SU (2)1/SU(2)k+1. Ward like identities can be used for rational conformal field theories or correlation functions. The Knizhnik Zanrolodchikos Relation gives explicit expression of correlation functions where

$$k\frac{\partial}{\partial zi} - \sum j = \frac{\bar{i}\,ti^{atj^a}}{zi} - zj)\ <,\ g(z1, z'1) \ldots g(zn, z'n) \geq 0\ where\ i$$

doesn't equal j and i is the initial event and j is the final event.

In terms of Conformal Field Theories which measure mass in terms of conformal gravity we find the Super-conformal Minimal Series |h+->=S+-(0)|0>where |h->=Go|h+>where |0>is the bosonic vacuum state S+-(Z) is the spin field the conformal field is *$\phi h(z, 0)$ and $/h \geq \phi h(0,0)|0 >$ where the highest weight vacuum $|h >$ is annihilated by the generators with positive indicies. The vacuum state is a Fermionic field where $|h+->$ is a fermion. $\Gamma = (-1)^F$ where F = Fermion number. Vacuum divided to $\Gamma|h\pm\geq\pm|h\pm>$ where $\{\Gamma, G n\} = \{\Gamma, Ln\} = 0$. G 0 is the ground state of energy with regard to conformal gravity and $G0^2 = L0 - \frac{c}{16}$ where $\frac{G}{H} = \frac{SU(2)kxSU(2)2}{SU(2)k} + 2$ in Yang Mills Format* where H is a primary conformal field Hamiltonian for k to n eigenstates of energy. In the 2 dimensional lattice Ising Model Equation the conformal weight *Δ of the field whose energy operator products $\epsilon n = \sigma n \sigma n + 1$ where σ = isospins from the energy field. $< \epsilon n \epsilon 0 \geq \frac{1}{x}$* $^{-2\left(d-\frac{1}{v}\right)}$ *where v and η are critical exponents for the Ising Model for the spin field and energy*

Where h+h′ are the Ising Fields 2 for Conformal Field whose Conformal Gravity is *Δ such that g ij = x^d + 2 - η where d = dimension which approximately equals $x^{-2\Delta}$ where the critical* exponents are $\eta = \frac{1}{4}$ and $\upsilon = 1$ so in the minimal model $= 3$ $\sigma =$ $\frac{\frac{\phi 1}{16,1}}{16}$ and $\epsilon = \frac{\frac{\phi 1}{2,1}}{2}$. In this case the mass gap $< \phi(0, t)\phi(0,0) \geq \Sigma nA$ n $e^{(-\Delta nt)}$ where g $ij = x^{-2\Delta}$ where $\Delta =$ conformal weight or mass. As g i $j = {}_x 2\Delta e^{-x(\in)}$ where $\in$ is the correlation length at cirat criticality goes to ∞ so e^{-x} ϵ becomes $\frac{1}{e\infty}$ or 0. This can be extended to d^4 and d^n which is the compactified n dimensions where $n<\infty$ utilizing g $ij=x^4\Delta e^{-4x(\epsilon)w}$ and applying the action formula on g ij where i=initial event and j=the final event which is at criticality or absolute zero. The action $(S)=-1/2k^2(-g)^{1/2}R$ ij which show the vibratory motion of photons according to the harmonic oscillator where the miniscule mass of $3x10^{-18}$ eV/c^2 is ~ 0 for photons but as it isn't 0 this accounts for the mass gap in Yang Mills AS THE U(1) subcategory for electromagnetic radiation pre-disposes that photons are massless which they aren't. THE ACTION FORMULA IN 26 DIMENSIONS IS S=-(minus one) $1/2k^2$

$\sqrt{d^{26(-g)ij(g)ji}}R$ ij (where R ij is the space – time curvature me variant of metric g ij) where g Zero (0) at critical temperature causes the system to lose all dependence on fundamental length and the mass gap or conformal gravity gap–Δn holds. This is the lowest energy in the spectrum of the Hamiltonian and photons at 0,1(1--) OR 1(I^pc) ARE THE NEXT LEVEL RENDERING FERMIONIC FIELD WITH PHOTONS AT CRITICAL LENGTH AND K EIGENSTATE FOR GROUND STATE AND K+1.. EIGENSTATE FOR ENERGY OF PHOTON $\epsilon 0\epsilon 1 = \Sigma K \rightarrow K + 1$ FOR $\epsilon 1$ PHOTON ENERGY STATE. D is expanded to to four dimensional Euclidian space in $x^{-2}(d-1/\upsilon)$ where $d =$ ¡ ^{4} rendering g ij $= \frac{x^{-2(¡^4-1)}}{\upsilon}$ where ¡ $^4 -\frac{1}{\upsilon}$ is conformal weight Δ in Euclidian 4 space and therefore the mass gap Δ where $\Delta > 0$, Therefore the U(1) subgroup of Yang Mills Theory must incorporate vibrating photons in a matrix of Boso-Einsteinian Condensate where the photons are still not at rest and still have non-resting mass of 10^{-18}ev/c^2. Of course, Boso-Einsteinian Condensate is a state which was discovered in 1995 by Dr. Lene Hau a Harvard Physicist 1. This extends the U(1) subgroup from criticality at absolute zero.

1. Wikipedia; Properties of Photons
2. Hau, Lene; Physicist Slows Speed of Light. Harvard Gazette 1999
3. Kaku, Michio. Superstrings Conformal Fields and, M Theory 2nd Edition Springer Press p. 168

Bibliography
123 1. ibid(footnote 1)
124 2. ibid(footnote 2)
125 3. ibid(footnote 3)

CHAPTER EIGHT

A SHORT ESSAY REGARDING THE EQUATION OF EVERYTHING

The short simple relationship in verbal terms space-time is directly proportional to space and inversely proportional to mass is in reality when converted to metric tensors an equation which compactifies to a circle as does type IIA string theory and possibly all five dual string theories comprising M Theory. This equation has over 500,000 permutations which may in all actuality be all the equations in Nature including those discovered and undiscovered.

THE TENSOR FORM OF SPACE-TIME=SPACE/MASS

Space-time constricts as in Schwarzchild Space-time as the event horizon of any active black hole is approached. Black holes are extremely dense with extremely compressed mass and the gravitational effect or perturbation is extreme causing the observer to note a "frozen" image in time in as much the the event horizon appears to be dilated time(time slowing down near heavy masses)with the constrictive effect of progressively increasing space-time curvature as the event horizon is being approached although an infinite curvature point of space-time is never reached(asymptotic). Space-time is inversely proportional to mass.

Based on the Line Element space-time or ds^2=dx^2+dy^2+dz^-c^2dt^2+dr^2 indicates that even with the Relativistic effect on the dimension of time noted by c^2dt^2 space-time is direclt proportional to space.

CHAPTER NINE

PHYSICAL COSMOLOGY; ISOTROPISM VS. AN ISOTROPISM OF OUT UNIVERSE

Based on the large scale distribution of mass and constraints on the large scale anisotropy (observational asymmetry) of the Background Microwave Radiation $\dfrac{\delta T}{T} \sim 10^{-5\,mwit}$ *hthe velocity field being 30 h MParsecs and the clustering of galaxies and mass.*

The Sacks-Wolfe Relation (1967) has the CBR temperature inversely proportional to temp in degrees kelvin. The δ *h is measured orthogonally* to indicate quadruple anisotropy $\delta\frac{T}{T} = \delta$ *h where t 0 > 10^4 such that the large scale expansion appears to be close to isotropic. The Newtonian potenti*

Energy due to gravity is $\phi \sim \dfrac{G\delta m}{a} x = \dfrac{\frac{G}{a} x \delta m}{m} \dfrac{4}{3\pi} = \rho\, B(ax)^3 = \dfrac{1}{2\Omega H^{2(ax)^2}}$

. δ x or 0.5 Ω $(H^{2(ax)^2\delta x} \cdot \dfrac{\delta m}{m} = \delta x^{aa(t)}$. *That is* $\dfrac{dm}{m} = \delta x^a\,(a(t).$

With the Einstein deSitter Limit expansion scale ay H α to $a\frac{3}{2}$ or H is directly proportional to a relating to the expansion to the $\frac{3}{2}$ power the Gravitational potential energy due to mass fluctuations ϕ are independent of time. This is because the density constant indicating homogeneity of this universe grows at $\dfrac{\delta m}{m} = \delta x^{aa(t)w}$

49

hereby a(t) indicates Hubble Time and delta $\frac{m}{m}$ is the change in mass over Hubble Time.

This incorporate the all important spiral fractal formula of $\int \frac{du}{u}$ *where u = mass and the limits relate to Hubble Time. The gravitational redshift* $\delta \frac{v}{v} \sim \phi$ *and there are* perturbations to the CBR temperature. CBR anisotropy is caused by mass density fluctuations and like perturbations to the CBR temperature. This relates to a co-moving scale at Hubble distance (x). So $\frac{\delta T}{T} \sim$ $(H0a0x)^{2\delta x(0)}$ *with a potential as being k. The avg length is Hubble Length or a1x.* $\frac{\delta T}{T} \sim \delta x(0)$

On an angular scale this boundary goes down to fractions of seconds of arc where one second is 1/3600 degree. 2 This results in the Sachs-Wolfe Relation decreasing with a decreasing scale with respect to δx. *Thus the CBR anisoropy shrinks on the angular scale as subdivisions reduce toward second of arc.* However over time these fluctuations may not be totally time independent and the clumpiness may change due to the anti-gravitational effect of the cosmologic constant flattening out space-time. Still as the expansive component continues to expand geometrically and the rotational component from the Big Bang reduces significantly due to Regee Slope Trajectories homogeneity appears to increase with time an anisotropism becomes more difficult to detect which is why gravity waves must be used to measure space-time curvature to locate the supermassive black hole as the location of the Big Bang and the center of mass in what appears to be an only slightly anisotropic universe. If there is no center of mass in our universe due to ISOTROPY that means that A Big Bang COULD NOT OCCUR IF IT DOESN'T ORIGINATE FROM A POINT IN SPACE. Since the syllogism that the Big Bang cannot originate from any point in space it's a false syllogism. Does this mean that there wasn't a Big Bang? The accelerating expansion of our universe can be caused by space-time pulling space-time as a current outward in all directions and the pulling space-time traveling at 2.2x10^35(c)meters/sec can be pulling our local space-time toward the center of a vortex from the outward position of the vortex where space-time is almost totally flat (5x10^-29 radians). If dark energy is pushing space-time and space-time is pulling space-time in the same Cartesian coordinates there doesn't have to be an origin point to expansion the accelerating expansion of this universe. This gives some volition to the "Steady State Theory" which was eclipsed

by "The Big Bang" however the FIRST EVENT OR THE INFINITE PARALLEL PLANE HYPOTHESIS STILL HOLDS FORMING A VORTEX WITH OUT UNIVERSE BEING ON THE PERIPHERY FORMING FROM STRINGS. DESPITE THIS, THIS AUTHOR IS STILL AGNOSTIC ABOUT THIS UNIVERSE BEING TOTALLY ISOTROPIC AND HOMOGENEOUS AS THERE MAY BE MEASURING DEFECTS IN THE RED SHIFTS AS THERE ARE NO CLEAR DIRECTIONS WHERE THE RED SHIFTS ARE GRAVITATING TO. EITHER THERE WAS A BIG BANG AND OUR UNIVERSE HAS A CENTER OF MASS AND A ROUNDED CIRCULAR EDGE OR THERE WAS NO BEGINNING SINCE THE FORMATION OF STRINGS AS THE FIRST EVENT. Our universe is near the outer periphery of the space-time continuum due to the flatness of space-time in our universe. This means that the pulling effect from spacetime in the vortex towards the center of the vortex or it's center of mass is not as strong as it will be as the center of the vortex is approached. The vortex is so huge that at the periphery a center of mass cannot be detected with our technology and with the miniscule curvature of our space-time at 5x10^-29 radians we note the expansion due to the space-time current and dark energy plus homogeneity and isotropism as the center of mass of the system is the center of the vortex which is almost an infinite distance away from us. Based on that our clinical observations could show that our universe may have been formed from string right after the First Event without a Big Bang although Inflation is still possible. The degree of space-time curvature for an entire universe can be utilized as a partition function relative to the total space-time curvature of the space-time continuum(which is spiral asymptotic to a cone comprised of a confluence of an infinite number of 2-D-spheres or flat hyper-spherical surfaces progressive decreasing in diameter from an infinite diameter with flat space-time curvature to a point of infinite space-time curvature.)Considering a total space-time curvature of our universe as 5x10^-29 radians as compared to an almost infinite amount of space approaching but never reaching 0 radians; space-time curvature CAN LOCATE THE RELATIVE POSITION OF ANY UNIVERSE IN THE SPACE-TIME CONTINUUM AS LONG AS THE DEGREE OF SPACE-TIME CURVATURE OR FLATNESS FOR EACH SEGMENT OF THE SPACE-TIME CONTINUUM CAN BE DETERMINED. The center of the vortex has approaching infinite curvature and the extremes have virtually no curvature so a plot of space-time curvature versus relative position can be created. It would make sense that any "vacuum universes" with totally or almost totally flat space-time would be at or near the periphery of the space-time continuum. In the event of the existence of the multi-verse one must know the composition of each universe and mass to determine it's particular space-time curvature and therefore locate its position,

9.2 WHAT IF THERE WAS NO RELATIVE POSITION FOR A BIG BANG?

In order to have a homogeneous isotropic universe with no center of mass then any Big Bang would have either occurred everywhere or would have to keep banging throughout the expansion at every possible site in space-time. The mass distribution has a constraint of the Sachs-Wolfe Effect mentioned earlier. Mass fluctuations $\frac{\delta M}{M}$, $< 10^{-4}$. *Over ∞ volume the mass fluctuations in the mass distribution becomes the Hubble Length*

4000 Mega parsecs as a boundary to L H or Hubble Length. The mass fluctuations are ~ 1 when what's termed the smoothing radius (the central path with reference to Hubble length) is reduced to 1% of Hubble Length where dl/dt=H 0 (l) where l is the mean distance between conserved particles which increases with time at H 0(l). H 0 is the Hubble Constant L h(Hubble Length)=c/H 0 $\sim$ 4000 Megaparsecs. The recession velocity of the expansion extrapolates to "c" or 3x10^ 8 m/sec which is actually in space-time traveling in all directions at *πc in every and all directions while being pulled at* $2.2x10^{35(c)}$ *by the current of space – time heading toward the middle of the vortex formed with the Infinite Parallel Planes.*

As the Big Bang is an identifying event triggering an explosions it suggested the event must have occurred in space. If the universe has no center of mass there is no localized explosion in space and the only physical evidence that exists for this is the background microwave radiation and the WOMP which illustrated some clumpiness. There is no clear evidence that any site of the explosion had a localized center, As a consequence the is only soft evidence that such an event actually happened. This indicates that after the Time Oscillation Paradox acted on the Infinite Parallel Planes strings formed matter and anti-matter after the spin2 vector bosons occurred. This indicates that after the time oscillation acted on the infinite parallel planes that there wasn't an explosion but perhaps Inflation or a mutual repulsion between anti-particles which pushed matter and a scintilla of anti-matter outward in all discernable directions from everywhere. Of course this pre-supposed that the anti-matter may homogeneously distributed throughout the matter which caused a sequestration of the anti-matter and matter at opposite poles at a fracture point with a symmetric throat at the 0,0 point. So as a consequence either there was no Big Bang or this universe of ours has a center of mass and a discernible location in space where the Big Bang occurred. It was postulated by this author that there is a supermassive black hole not yet discovered by space-time curvature measurements which is the center of mass and that this universe is not totally isotropic and homogeneous. If this wasn't the case the formation of strings formed either the entire multiverse or just one universe which pushed out in all directions from any scintilla of anti-matter after the anti-matter was formed.

9.3 OCCAM'S RAZOR (does it help?)

The scientific precept of Occam's Razor (Ockham's Razor) states that all things being equal the simplest explanation tends to be the right one. So what is more likely, that our universe has no center of mass or gravity when it has a mass of 10^{64} kg and that a quantum bubble (containing everything) appeared out of absolutely nothing and exploded in all directions with the explosion no point of origin in space creating a universe with no edge or the universe has a supermassive black hole which hasn't been discovered yet where the rotational vector originated before the expansion and that the universe rotated around that central axis while expanding geometrically. Normally the answer should be the latter however part of Occam's Razor also states "all things being equal" which means that there aren't outside systems acting into the equation with missing data and information. An example of this is the equation 345+-----=7----. What's the answer; insufficient data. With insufficient data even in a minimum information problem it still doesn't compute with one answer. As one doesn't know if the sum is 7,70,71,700,750,7000,7546....all the way out to 7(infinite number of digits there are an infinite number of solutions so there is insufficient data). In this equation all things aren't equal. Also the precept of an intelligent or non-intelligent observer must be present and changes reality also flunks Occam's Razor but the observer means "all things aren't equal". Sadly there may still be "insufficient data" like the addition problem to determine the correct solution.

"The Omega Point "was postulated by Frank Tipler Ph.D. as that point whereby everything learnable is learned. As the storage capacity of our brains is probably under that; an individual is unlikely to reach that, however a Turing Test positive automaton with deca-byte or decillion-byte storage capacity may. As only a small percentage of the equations in nature have been discovered or derived approximately 25% scientists have a long road a head of them to fill in the "insufficient data" to answer every question in nature. It may take this to determine the full scope of any and all outside systems acting upon nature.

9.4 WAS THE BIG BANG A BIG SWIRL?

The rotational component of the two sequestered poles of matter and anti-matter was maximum at Planck Time 10^{-43} seconds.. If the ORIGINAL POINT WAS THE CENTER OF THE VORTEX FORMED WITH THE TIME OSCILLATION PARADOX AND IF STRINGS(including matter and anti-matter)initially swirled outward in every direction from this site with the anti-gravitational moment of anti-particle antiparticle repulsion emerging from the extreme sequestration of the spin2 vector bosons from that site after the formation of string dimensions coupled with the annihilation of matter and anti-matter negating the possible anti-gravitational effect of matter and anti-matter this combined force swirling outward at 2π *radians there* May have been sufficient force to propel our universe outward to the periphery of the vortex of spiral space-time prior to the expansion pull of space-time back toward the center of the vortex. This would be a modified spring effect but as our universe doesn't seem to reflect a bouncing effect or a recoil and since the directions would be 180 degrees from the direction back towards the center of the vortex the expansion MUST BE A RECOIL EFFECT FROM THE SPRING EFFECT OF THE BIG SWIRL OR BANG. As a consequence the location of this universe in the space-time continuum would be the MAXIMUM DISTANCE that the spring effect propelled matter and energy prior to the extreme pull of space-time back towards the center of the vortex. The only contrary evidence to this idea is that the velocity of the expansion reveals no deceleration prior to the accelerated expansion of 6.75x10^34 erg. and the accelerated expansion would be π *radians or* 180 *degrees from the inital spring effect*. This concept was in this author's first book "Mega-physics: A New Look at the Universe" and there may have been 700 googoplex of similar events with different configuration or similar configurations to that of our universe including an anti-swirl corresponding to out swirl either cohabiting the same space with a phase shift explaining overlap phenomena which can't easily be explained such as paranormal phenomena or may inhabit different space entirely. This also was discussed in this author's first book "Mega-physics, A New Look at the Universe" and this anti-swirl phenomenon would absorb any deceleration of the accelerated expansion after Planck Time by moving in the opposite direction with the same or similar magnitude. The unaccounted for mass as described by dark matter(made of baryonic particles, neutrinos, WIMPS and other "stuff" which acts as a cosmic glue) may be heterotic in nature;flipping between dimensions with the odd dimensions being directly measurable(ordinary matter) and the even dimensions only indirectly measurable(dark matter with a mass=mass of ordinary matter/i). These even dimensions may reflect with the antiswirl component of either our universe or a parallel universe coexisting in the same dimensional matrix. The 1-brane and

2-brane reflect electric charge, the electron(or positron) and it's spread or distribution as that also of any electromagnetic radiation. The 3-brane and 4-brane reflect space for ordinary matter(3 dimensional) and "flat" or 2 dimensional matter where the third dimension is string sized as in the photon. The 3- brane would reflect space for photons, etc and the 5-brane may contain dark matter with a hybrid mass which oscillates between + and – but isn't + or – making it's direct measurement very difficult except via higher gravitational measurement than projected mathematically. In the book "Megaphysics II: An Explanation of Nature" this author described dark matter as the cosmic residue from burned out anti-matter from the Big Bang like a match with phosphors being the matter and anti-matter the striking being the Big Bang and the charcoal residue on the tip of the match being dark matter. During a phase shift(see" Megaphysics:,A New Look at the Universe")it may be possible to DIRECTLY MEASURE DARK MATTER as well as any other phenomena among other dimensions including paranormal phenomena. As mentioned in the book "Megaphysics,;A New Look at the Universe" the inertial mass from the missing mass including dark matter should have slowed the accelerated expansion down, which it didn't so as a consequence the additional gravity or curvature of space-time caused by the inertial mass must be severely affected by the properties of that inertial mass. If the inertial mass doesn't slow down the acceleration it may not be in our universe or at least part of the inertial mass may not be in our universe and as a hybrid it would be the –mass oscillation that exists either in shadow dimensions or a shadow universe. The perception of our brain records images through the eye which are inverted and reduced(real images)and the brain flips them upright and adjusts the size. In the same scope, the measuring devices of inertial mass must be able to measure ALL MASS even hybrid or oscillating heterotic mass.

CHAPTER TEN

HOW THE EQUATION PF EVERYTHING APPLIES TO THE BIG BANG

R abcd(n)= 2! + !!"!→!

!!"#! → i + 2π(R abc + or − !

!! g !"

! or − ih Λ ba + ρ ab. *In the case of The Big Bang as a spring effect with a countercurrent in space time from the from the center of the vortex of space – time out toward the relative location of our universe in the vortex the spiral operator reahes* reaches zero when the spring was exausted before the accelerated expansion back towards the center of the vortex. This is shown as 2^n+1πω i → j *goes from* ∞ *to* 0 *and* 2nπω j→ i *goes from* 0 *to* ∞ *making an infintie number of constants except* 0 *totalling up to the infinite* product of 0. The n eigen-state of curved Lorenzian or Riemannian Space-time has flat eucidian space with gravity and anti-gravity effect divided by the energy equivalent to inertial mass or R ab=ℏρ ab or ℏ(Λ ba + ρ ab) where ℏ = $h\frac{}{2\pi}$ and h = *Planck's Constant. The square root of – 1 or i relates to the Wave Function in the Schrodinger Equation and the = + or – i relates to the heterotic property as in the Wick Rotation. The 0 eigenstate at the center of the* vortex relates the the near infinite string dimensions after the Time Oscillation Paradox acting on the Infinite Number of Parallel Planes. In this case 2^n=1 times pi times angular momentum going from the final state j to the initial state i=1/

pi(omega)j.2^n+1=2 so 2(pi)omega I to j/(pi)(omega j to i=2(net total angular momentum). The net angular momentum omega I to j/omega j to i approaches zero. So in the zero dimensional state before the time oscillation paradox the angular momentum was zero but approaches infinity after the time oscillation paradox as the angular momentum goes from approaching zero to approaching infinity with energy as 10^77 joules forming from nearly 100% potential energy into potential and kinetic energy. Planck's Constant is the energy level of electromagnetic radiation divided by the frequency of the electromagnetic radiation and therefore IS THE CORRECTION BETWEEN INERTIAL MASS AS DESCRIBED BY R ab or the Ricci Tensor and the energy density of matter ρ ab +Λ ba which is the energy density of a vacuum. As the deBroglie Equation states wave-length=h/mass (velocity) or h/mass (speed of light) but it states that every wave function has an associated frequency and wavelength associated with its respective mass related by Planck's Constant. The energy density of a vacuum is described by the Cosmologic Constant before the time oscillation paradox and by the energy density of matter plus the cosmologic constant after the time oscillation paradox and the energy density of matter approaches 10^77 joules after the spring from the center of the vortex approaches the relative location of out universe in the space-time continuum. When the spring exhausted and the acceleration of space-time as a current began approaching the center of the vortex. The expansion of the universe is occurring in CONSTRICTING SPACE-TIME AS IT APPROACHES THE CENTER OF THE VORTEX MAKING THE EXPANSION APPEAR TO BE GREATER THAN IT ACTUALLY IS FROM THE STANDPOINT OF THE OBSERVER who is part of the system that is expanding with increasing flattening of space-time within a vortex of constricting increasing curvature space-time so the effect is flattening or increasing curvature of space-time within and without the system in the larger system makes another current or countercurrent in space-time dampening the accelerated expansion toward the center of the vortex. As this dampening effect continues over time the expansion may continue to decrease and stop eventually ending in Heat Death (Frank Tipler Ph.D. The Anthropic Cosmologic Principle) or even a Big Crunch.

CHAPTER ELEVEN

THE REGION OF SPACE-TIME OF THE PRIMORDIAL BLACK HOLE AND THE SITE OF THE BIG BANG

R=Region of space-time R abcd=Region of space-time which is curved R abc=Region of space-time which is flat. In the case of the Big Bang the region of space-time is the center of the vortex of space-time formed from the first event. This region has infinite curvature and is constricted towards zero without reaching it. As a result R abcd in the first eigen-state is constricted to 0 with infinite curvature resulting in the equation as R abcd(1)=0 and R g ab=∞ *as R g ab is the curvature of space – time caused by mass.* Total curved space-time=total flat space-time+ or – space-time curvature metric/mass doing the curving. In the case of the primordial black hole Rabcd(1)=∞=Rabc+∞ *(infinite curvature)/∞(infinite mass)*=everything except zero. Curved space-time which is constricted toward zero has infinite curvature from gravity with near infinite mass in the space-time continuum. This presumes that the space-time continuum after the first event had infinite mass and infinite gravity rather than finite mass and finite gravity. As a consequence EVERYTHING EXCEPT ZERO (space-less-ness) is R abcd in the first eigen-state after the first event reveals infinitely curved space-time constricted in the case of the center of the vortex of the space-time continuum where the effect of gravity approaches infinity as does the mass which must be the total mass as infinity/infinity=everything except zero. The spiral operator at i=initial event must be the center as the inifinite product of the numerator is 2^n+1$\pi\omega$ $i \to i$ where $n = 1$ (*the eigenstate after the first event*). $2^n + 1 = 2^2 = 4$. *This becomes Poisson's* Equation ($\tilde{N}(\omega, \rho[\tau]) = 4\pi\rho$(*total*); as the result of the numerator which is an expanding spiral operator is 4 $\pi\rho$ *where ρ is the energy density of matter. So as a consequence the angular momentum* Is initially the energy density of matter. The dual vector field is ρ, ω *where ρ is the energy density of matter and ω is angular momentum. Stress Energy T ab* 4$\pi r\rho$(2) *as ρ(R g ab) + ρ(R ab) where R g ab is gravity and R ab is inertia reveals the stress energy tensor times 8πor???* This added to everything except zero and the result is clearly the entirety of the curved space-time continuum WITHOUT SPACE-LESS-NESS OR NOTHING WHICH DOESN'T EXIST. 8πT *is the solution to Einstein's Equation of Relativistic Gravity.*

CHAPTER TWELVE

INFORMATION EXCHANGE VIA SPOOKY ACTION AT A DISTANCE

As the solution to the Hawking Paradox is the transmission of information from a dissolving black hole event horizon like a suspension in fluid space-time like tang in water or Na Cl in water; yet Spooky Action at a Distance between photon pairs of electrons with regard to spin or charge can be over vast distances. Can this dissemination of information between electron "gasses" which spread out ad infinitum also apply to the dissemination of information from the event horizons of black holes also. If that is so the THERE WILL BE AN INFORMATION EXCHANGE BETWEEN BLACK HOLES JUST AS THERE ARE BETWEEN ELECTRONS OR PHOTONS AT GREAT DISTANCES. How can one prove that the information in one black hole contains the information in another black hole? If this is true the information from the supermassive black hole at the site of the Big Bang can be "smeared" throughout space-time and concentrated at the event horizon of other closer black holes. The answer is still gravity waves or changes in space-time curvature. Examining the ideal space-time curvature according to Schwarzchild Space-time of any black hole and comparing it with measured perturbations in space-time curvature according to the LIGO project will give a minute difference where Schwarzchild Space-time is calculated and LIGO space-time is measured. The difference is a perturbation due to information gathering from other black holes including the supermassive black hole at the Big Bang which shows more curvature due to the increased rotational moment than other black holes.

MATH CHAPTER 12.2

Space-time or R abcd(n) is -1/2 e^-in cot θ *which when the spiral operator is applied as* 2^n + $1\pi\omega$ *i* $\rightarrow \dfrac{j}{2^{n\pi\omega} j} \rightarrow$ *i has the information from a dissolving black hole as Hawking Radiation spuming as a quasa*

Hawking Radiation relates to the Unruh Effect 3 and the equivalence principle with respect to Black Hole Event Horizons. The Schwarzchild Black Hole metric is ds^2=(1-2M/r)dt^2+1/1-(2M/r) dr^2+2r^2dΩ^2 *with the Unruh Effect as the Temperature =* $\dfrac{1}{2\pi\rho} = 1/4\pi\sqrt{2m(r-2m)}$. *In other words As objects fall into a black hole the observer feels accelerate*

In Minkowski space (flat) by the Equivalence Principle. The gravitational redshift is the square-root of the metric of space-time curvature. Utilizing the Stefan-Boltzman Constant $\sigma = \dfrac{\pi^{2k^{4\beta}}}{60} h^{3c^2}$ *the Schwarzchild Radius of Black Hole event horizons is r(s)=* $\dfrac{2GM}{c^2}$ *and Black Hole Surface Gravity is g =* $\dfrac{GM}{r^{2(s)}} = \dfrac{c^4}{4GM}$ *and the corresponding energy is* h$\dfrac{g}{2\pi c}$ = h$\dfrac{1}{2\pi c \left(\frac{c^4}{4GM}\right)}$ = h$\dfrac{c^3}{8\pi GM}$ *for Hawking Radiation. The peak weavelength of Hawking Radiation is 16 times the Sch???*

The peak wave length of Hawking Radiation is almost 16 times the Schwarz child Radius of a Black hole. The equation is λ *max =* $\left(\dfrac{8\pi^2}{4.9651}\right)$ r(s) = 15.902 r(s) where r(s) *is* the Schwarzchild *Radius* of a black hole event horizon and the wavelength of Hawking Radiation relates to flat Minkowski Space-time as ds^2=dx^2+dy^2=dz^2-c^2dt^2 from the line element. With regard to Spooky Action at a Distance Hawking Radiation is electromagnetic radiation perturbing space-time in a spiral configuration so the spiral operator $2n+1^\wedge \pi\omega\, i \to j$ (*for expanding space – time from a point to flat space – time for Hawking Radiation to perturb space – time toward the adjacent black hole event horizons where space – time constricts by the spiral operator to* $\dfrac{1}{2^{n\pi\omega}\, j} \to i$ *and the angular momentum increases geometrically as the event horizon of all other* black holes are approached. The energy of Hawking Radiation is *$\rho(H)$ in the Equation of Everything is $i\hbar\rho(H)$ so that $2\pi(R\ abc\ +$ or $-\frac{1}{2}R\, g\frac{ab}{i}\, h\rho(H)$ and $\Sigma\rho(H) = \lambda$ max or the peak wavelength which is the reciprocal of the frequency υ which relates to the en energy* of Hawking Radiation. As photon pairing is electromagnetic radiation and is subject to Spooky Action at a Distance photons also follow the paths of space-time curvature in the same way as other types of electromagnetic radiation as all are comprised of photons including Hawking Radiation.

Utilizing the formula for space-time as -1/2e-I n cot(theta) where theta is the trajectory of Hawking Radiation the trajectory is 90 degrees or $\dfrac{\pi}{2}$ radians which is $\cos\dfrac{\frac{\pi}{2}}{\frac{sin\pi}{2}}$ which is $\dfrac{0}{1}$ or 0. *This is consistant with the constriction of space – time towards zero at the event horizon of any active black hole. Thus $= \dfrac{1}{2}e^{-in(0)}$ wheren is the two dimensional state relating to the flat matter of Hawking Radiation $e^\wedge 0=1$ and $1/2e^\wedge 0=1/2$ while $-1/2e^\wedge 0=-1/2$ so the midpoint is the inception of a self* contained LOOP OF HAWKING RADIATION IN CONSTRICTED TO DILATED SPACE-TIME FROM THE EVENT HORIZON OF ONE BLACK HOLE TO THE EVENT HORIZON OF ANOTHER BLACK HOLE. THIS IS TOTALLY CONSISTANT WITH TOTAL INFORMATION

EXCHANGE OF HAWKING RADIATION BETWEEN EACH AND EVERY BLACK HOLE WHERE TIME ISN'T IMPORTANT AS HAWKING RADIATION GOES FROM CONSTRICTED SPACE-TIME OF ONE BLACK HOLE WITH DILATED TIME TO CONSTRICTED SPACE-TIME WITH DILATED TIME OF ANOTHER BLACK HOLE THEREFORE THE INFORMATION DISBURSED INTO SPACE-TIME AS EITHER A SUSPENSION (where the 2 dimensional lattice formula can be applied) or if the information is dissolved in space-time and may travel in a formulation similar two the Robinson Congruence (which is a superfast pathway for photons which comprise electromagnetic radiation). These phenomena also explain photon pairing as a form of Spooky Action at a Distance. The phenomena involving spooky action with electrons was described in this author's second book "The Equation of Everything". 12.3 AN M THEORY APPROACH TO HAWKING RADIATION Assuming that Hawking Radiation is comprised of electromagnetic radiation or photons which are flat or two dimensional matter this would be associated with the 3-Brane associated with two dimensional space, the 4- Brane associated with three dimensions of space where the third dimension of photons would be string sized or 10^{-33} cm. The gathering or distribution of charge in the 2-Branes are generally associated with electrons which also has electromagnetic radiation as magnetism is formed from electromagnetic radiation as electrons are transferred as well as positrons(anti-electron)and the fact that photons have a miniscule mass would cause them to smear along multiple membranes or Branes as the velocity of electromagnetic radiation would only vary at just above absolute zero when photons vibrate in a lattice of Boso-Einsteinian condensate. Space itself would be comprised of leptons and gluons and photons would pass through the fabric of leptons as long as the gluons remained intact holding the leptons together and would therefore form the 4-Brane,5-Brane,....N-Brane all the way to the super-small Super-brane There were 252 separate states of matter in the average active black hole according to Stephen Hawking and black hole entropy $S=2(pi)(Q1Q5)^{1/2}$ *where N = number of states Q1 and Q5 are the differential charges.* Spooky Action between black holes would have space altered such that the 3 Brane would compress toward the superbrane constricting the volume of photons which would increase the volume geometrically BY THE MUZZLE EFFECT AS WITH A WATER BLAST IN A MUZZLE. CONSIDER ELECTROMAGNETIC RADIATION AS A PERFECT GAS WITH THE PERFECT FLUID OF SPACE-TIME;CONSTRICTING THE PERFECT GAS ENOUGH WILL INCREASE THE VELOCITY TO EXCESS OF 3×10^8 meters. sec as the velocity of space-time would also increase geometrically with constriction nd the photon stream of Hawking Radiation would constrict with the constricting space-time. Therefore photons would constrict to sizes which are virtually immeasurably small and immeasurably fast in the massive Super-brane explaining Spooky Action at a Distance for Hawking Radiation using M Theory.

FOOTNOTES;
1. Kaku, Michio. Introduction to Superstrings and M Theory p.61-62 and section 1.8 Harmonic Oscillator
2. Peebles. Principles of Physical Cosmology p.500-503
3. Wikipedia. Hawking Radiation.

CHAPTER THIRTEEN

WHAT IS MORE LIKELY THAT THE BIG BANG WAS PRECEDED BY A BIG CRUNCH

AND WAS NOT THE SECOND EVENT BUT HAPPENED AEONS LATER OR THAT THE BIG BANG WAS THE SECOND EVENT FOLLOWING THE FORMATION OF STRINGS, STRING DIMENSIONS AND MATTER?

Utilizing Occam's Razor the first explanation appears on the surface to be more plausible as it is logical and simple, however, is it? The second explanation would place the site of the Big Bang at the center of the vortex formed by the Time Oscillation Paradox acting on the infinite parallel planes of space. In order for the second explanation to be more correct would have to illustrate a recoil effect or spring effect in the opposite direction from the Big Bang which initially went outward in all directions from the center of the spiral vortex of space-time which had been previously formed. This spring effect would have had a deceleration early on after The Big Bang after which time the acceleration outward in all directions would have been a pull from space-time acting on space-time from our universe as a current along with the push of dark energy which is a relatively weak force of anti-gravity. In other words there was a push outward from Dark Energy from the mutual repulsion of anti-particles in the quantum bubble from the center of the vortex but this push was almost IMMEDIATELY overtaken by the pull of space-time back toward the center of the vortex causing the accelerated expansion toward the center of the vortex. Note immediately could be anything from Planck Time or 10^-43sec to several hundred thousand years. The answer is in the data. If the WOMP or any studies of gravity waves or measurements of space-time curvature would show a change or reversal in the acceleration early on followed by a substantial increase in the acceleration. As a consequence, with the knowledge our technology has the conclusion must be soft or tenuous at best albeit possible. Theo other alternative which is simpler and easier to explain is a Big Crunch of another universe with space-time constricting toward zero and time dilating toward infinity (infinitely slow relative to the observer) which would mean the progressive dilation of time would slow either slow it toward zero from positive time moving progressively slower until time 0 is approached as the quantum bubble is formed in constricted space-time or time would move backwards from positive toward zero in a negative direction as in the case of a massive IMPLOSION. In this case The Big Bang was certainly not the second event but occurred much much later. Of course the collision of membranes could also have caused it but of course this too would mean it isn't the second event but would have happened much much later. So what is correct? Are all things equal? If science can answer that question we will be considerably closer to the OMEGA POINT. To learn all things that are learnable would answer the question "When are all things equal?". Until then the first statement toward wisdom is "I don't know".

13.2 ANTIPARTICLE ANTIPARTICLE REPULSION AS CAUSE OF THE BIG BANG

IN A SYMMETRICAL 360 DEGREE ORB BLAST AT THE BIG BANG R^ijkl=antigravity effect on particles and Rji^kl is the antigravity effect on antiparticles. $\Lambda ij = 1/Rij^2 = 1/8\pi G$ where $R\,ji$ = antigravity from antiparticles $\dfrac{1}{Rij^2\,is}$ spacetime from the Cosmologic Constant. The vector prod $Rij^2 \ddot{A} R\,ji$ reveals $R^{2ijRji}/|Rij^2||Rji = cos\theta$ which reveals that $e\,ji\dfrac{R^{2ijR}\,ji}{\left\|R^{2ij}\right\|}$ $||Rji||$ where $0 < \theta < \pi$ radians. In a symmetrical orb blast the re are an infinite number of slices with a total trajectory of π radians. The cosine of π radians is – 1. so $R\,ji = \dfrac{1}{8\pi G \otimes g}ij$ The vector product of $Rij(R\,ji) = e(ij, ji)cos\theta$. $Rij^{2(R\,ji)} = 1$. For π radians $R\,ji = -e\,ji$. As $g\,ij$ is the metric of a particle and – eji – is spacetime curvature or gravity of $R\,ji$. $g\,ji$ is the metric of the antiparticle. $R\,ijkl$ is spacet

Time for antimatter in four dimensions and kl is positive space-time. With R jikl=covariant tensor and Rji^kl being the contra-variant tensor R ji=-e ji and R jikl- Rji^kl=-eji=g ji/8(pi)G where R jikl-R ji^kl is the space-time curvature from anti-matter, R jikl-R ji^kl=-8πG eji = g ji where g ji is the Riemann metric for an antiparticle and – 8πG is the ANTIGRAVITY FOR ANTIPARTICLES IN ANTIMATTER ILLUSTRATING A MUTUALLY

REPULSIVE FORCE. R ijkl is space-time curvature for gravity and R jikl is space=time curvature or reciprocal curvature for antigravity and of course g ij is the metric for particles with positive gravity and g ji is the metric for the anti-particle with anti-gravity. Finally R ^ijkl is the antigravity effect on particles and R ji^kl is the antigravity effect on antiparticles which forms the - 8 πG which is the multiplier of e ji to equal the metric g ji which is the metric of the antiparticle

Clearly the negative sign illustrates anti-gravity for anti-particles.

13.3: EVERY ACTION MUST HAVE AN EQUAL BUT OPPOSITE REACTION

According to Sir Isaac Newton every action must have an equal but opposite reaction. The Big Bang ex nihilo breaks that law of motion; however with the spring effect of the quantum bubble from emerging strings and string dimensions from the center of the vortex of spiral space-time IS THE ACTION after the time oscillation paradox spuming out in all directions to the point of deceleration from the center of the vortex. This then reverses toward the center of the vortex again with the accelerated expansion of our universe. Again this is due to the enormous pull of space-time from the vortex on space-time and push of dark energy within our universe and is the REACTION.. The equal but opposite reaction to the expansion of our galaxies from the quantum bubble and Big Bang was the push of anti-particle anti-particle repulsion within the quantum bubble from the center of the vortex to the POINT OF REVERSAL OF THIS UNIVERSE BACK TOWARDS THE CENTER OF THE VORTEX OF SPACE-TIME. Of course a Big Crunch of another universe with the same space-time current as our universe would also obey Newton's Second Law.

Therefore the event of "creation" in all actuality occurred when the rogue tachyon (s) dropped to the speed of light initiating the time oscillation paradox on the infinite parallel planes or the D-0-Branes. Again it is unclear as to whether only one universe or the multiverse formed from the advent of string dimensions and strings as well as the spin 2 vector boson from the rogue tachyon(s) initiating gravity and converting almost 100% potential energy of the components of space into 10^{77} joules of kinetic energy after the paradox acted upon these infinite parallel planes spinning them into a centrifuge effect forming the vortex of space-time with matter gravitating towards the center as an origination point. THIS IS CLEARLY NOT OUT OF NOTHING AS NOTHING DOESN'T EXIST.

13.4 WAS THE ROGUE TACHYON COMPONET OF THE HIGGS FIELD (PRIOR TO THE FORMATION OF THE MASSIVE HIGGS BOSON) A PURPOSEFUL ACTION?

To mathematically determine if the rogue tachyon (s) was impelled by a conscious force (determinism vs. free will) is bringing together science and philosophy merging into religion and while K-suryon waves were determined to mathematically exist; it still hasn't been conclusively proven that consciousness is energy. Until that question is answered it will be unclear if creation was purposeful or random (which according to Quantum Mechanics would have a 100% probability with infinitely or nearly infinitely dilated time) for that event to occur. Chaos Theory would indicate randomness which follows the laws of entropy which would indicate that the most ordered state would be prior to the first event. Again if the vortex of space-time relates to the vortex of a black hole then the entropy would approach zero in the center of the vortex but not be zero. Stephen Hawking stated that black hole entropy approaches 0.29 and it is possible that the entropy of the quantum bubble would also approach that value in the center of the vortex of space-time with 252 disparate states of matter and space-time constricting towards zero without reaching it at the center (BEING THE LOCATION OF THE BIG BANG).

13.5 THE DISTRIBUTION OF SPACE-TIME AFTER THE FIRST EVENT

Space-time acts as a perfect fluid and the spiral configuration of the space-time continuum is like a giant whirlpool whose outer edges stretch out toward infinity in all directions from the center of the vortex. As the distance from the center of the vortex increases in all directions over 360 degrees the amount of curvature reduces until at the extremes (which are never met) space-time approaches absolute flatness which is like a stagnant pond. The quantum ground state as described by the spiral fractal formula is the ZERO DIMENSIONAL STATE and 100% potential energy-ϵ(*negligible kinetic energy*) *is ~ zero energy but is actually ε kineitic energy and* 100% $- \epsilon$ *potential energy from the components of space.* $\int_0^\pi \frac{du}{u} = \ln u \to 0$. VACUUM ENERGY IS THE SUM TOTAL OF THE POTENTIAL ENERGY OF SPACE WHICH IS COMPRISED OF LEPTONS AND BEING HELD TOGETHER BY MASSLESS GLUONS. IT CAN BE CONSIDERED AS 10^77 joules incurred by the Time Oscillation Paradox of the first event. Of course as mentioned in this author's previous book "What is the Dimension of Time?" time is the sequencing of events and without time all events would occur simultaneously in the same space which absolutely disallows space-less-ness as space-less-ness cohabiting space containing everything with sequencing would implode everything into space-less-ness which would require time as an implosion is an event as would be the formation of space from space-less-ness therefore they would have been nothing without time which can only be nothing and could have only been nothing WHICH IS NON-EXISTENCE therefore once again nothing doesn't exist and time does.

The classical definition of potential energy is P.E.=m g h where m=mass g=gravity and h=height. In the infinite planes hypothesis the height of the infinite planes is infinity. The mass of leptons is approaching mass-less-ness but still has a miniscule negligible mass and therefore negligible gravity which bleeds through from tachyons. Gravity is the curvature of space-time caused by mass, but the curvature of space is from time constricting or dilated space. If time is infinitely or nearly infinitely dilated the constrictions of space by time approaches ZERO so the pre-first event space is flat and totally parallel. As a consequence the negligible mass causing gravity cannot curve space with time completely dilated as it is time that is actually constricting space. As a result mass=ϵ *gravity = ϵ and space – time curvature = 0 as time is dilated. So the potential energy is $(\epsilon)(\epsilon)(\infty) = \infty$ and there is therefore ore ∞ (infinite) potential energy which released 10^{77} joules of kinetic energy* from the first event. Of course the Newtonian Definiton of Potential Energy as weight times height where weight is mass times gravity is only an approximation as it may not consider Relativistic effects on potential energy.

In terms of Metric Tensors Curved Riemannian or Lorenzian Space-time as a tensor of the fourth degree in n-dimensional space where n is from 1 toward infinity without reaching it. Riemann has 256 permutations between covariant and contravariant tensors with the Bianchi Identity applied and has the properties of being anti-symmetrical and Abelian.

This family of values is determined to be equal to a SPIRAL OPERATOR with regard to the function of Momentum producing a family of constants which are added to the equation of Flat Euclidian Space plus or minus the space-time curvature metric known as the effects of gravity and anti-gravity(which incorporates the Cosmologic Constant or the effects of Dark Energy. This value is the vector or tensor product of the reciprocal of inertial mass which is determined in this case by the Ricci Tensor.

The equation is

$R(n) = \prod$ (*from n=0 to a eigenstates of energy*) *of the spiral operator*

$(2^n+1)\pi P\ i \rightarrow \dfrac{j}{2^{n\pi P}\ j} \rightarrow i$ where i = *the initial event and j the final*

event indicating a bi – conal configuration which is asymptotic to a spiral operating on momentum (P) as heavy mass

Such as black holes in the denominator and toward the v=near vacuum of deep space and indicated in the numerator. These will result in a family of constants which are finite as eigen-state infinity is excluded as it results in the spiral operator zeroing out as an infinite curvature of a point as would only occur in an imploded universe such as a "Big Crunch".

This nearly infinite number of constants is added to R abc (flat Euclidian Space)+ or –1/2R g ab (space-time curvature metric or effect of gravity curving space-time inward and anti-gravity flattening space-time out such as the Cosmologic Constant being acted upon by the metric g (any measured quantity according to the Action Formula.) This is the dot product with regard to the reciprocal of the Ricci Tensor R ab which would normally be multiplied by a constant such as ~ $1/c^2$ to exactly form the Energy Density of Matter ρ ab. Due to the deBroglie Equation and equation for Planck's Energy R ab=$\hbar v(\rho\ ab)$. *As an energy level of a photon relates to frequency (v)* it can be incorporated into the energy density of matter as can the cosmologic constant which is the energy density of the near vacuum of space.

As $h = h\dfrac{}{2\pi}$ *the equation becomes* ¡ $(n)abcd = \prod \dfrac{n^{+1\pi\omega}}{n^{\pi\omega'}} + 2\pi(R$

abc + or $-\ \dfrac{1}{2}R\ g\dfrac{ab}{hv\rho}$ *as the Energy Density of matter times*

Planck's Constant *is in the denominator* and the 2π *goes into the numerator as* ℏ *becomes* $h\dfrac{}{2\pi}$.

The result is the equation of a Circle

Circumference=$2\pi R$ *where the circumference is space – time and the Radius is the sumtotal of all Riemann Forces of Nature. This is the compactified* (curled up) *form of at least type IIA Closed String Theory and perhaps all five String Theories which are mutually dual to each other form M-Theory which is Nature. The permutations or sub-equations to this relationship are enormous totaling at least 524,000 and if inclusive of the spiral operator acting on angular momentum* ω *may be in the trillions or more. As a conclusion the relationship space – time =* $\dfrac{space}{mass}$ *times a constant of* ~$\dfrac{1}{c^2}$ *has virutally all equations of Nature as permutations* which are 131,076(4)=~524,288 and may or may not be all the equations of Nature. Please note that the denominator ρ ab = R abℏ and *pab incorporates* Λ *ba which incorporate the energy density in a false vacuum of space. As* i ℏ *describes the wave function in the Schrodinger Equation the denominator must include* i *so*

$$\text{¡ } (n)abcd = \prod_0^\infty 2^n + 1\pi\omega i \rightarrow \frac{j}{2^{n\pi\omega}j} \rightarrow i\ 2\pi\left[R\,abc + or - \frac{1}{2}R\,g\,ab\right\} \otimes ih[\Lambda ba + \rho\ ab]$$

where Λ ba is incorporated into ρ ab as the energy density of matter and h = Planck's Constant. i = √−1. The compactification as a circle is circumference =space-time the radius is the sum of all Riemann Forces of Nature and the diameter is the sumtotal of all positive and negative Riemann Forces of Nature. Circumference=2πR *of is string theory (type IIA) or M –Theory which is the total of all five string theories type I, II, IIA, Heterotic 8x8 and the SO(32).* The spiral operator of the infinite product along 0 to infinity eigenstates of the expanding component of the component sphere or $2^\wedge(n+1)\pi\,i \rightarrow j$ *and the contracting compoent of circles from that of infinite diameter as in flat space – time and no curvature to a point with infinite curvature which is also the intersection of three*

Planes or $2^\wedge n\pi$ where the radius of the expanding and contracting circles forming the cone which is asymptotic to a spiral increasing or decreasing in diameter and radius. In this case the radius from the initial to the final event (i→ j) and the radius from the final to the initial event (j→ i) comprises an infinite number of constants in nature over an infinite number of eigenstates of energy and as the infinite product of the denominator goes to infinity the entire expression of the spiral operator goes to zero or vanishes from The Equation of Everything leaving Circumference (Curved Lorenzian or Riemannian Space-time)=2π *(total Riemannian Forces of Nature) as ℏ = h/2π and iℏ → ψ(r, t) or the wave function of point particle r at time t.*

CHAPTER FOURTEEN

WHAT IS HYPERSPACE?

Hyperspace is a continuum of points which are the intersection of three planes the xy, xz, yz where each intersection defines a point. There are an infinite number of points which are discontinuous and therefore hyperspace is discontinuous IF THE POINTS ARE STATIC; but as nothing is static as absolute zero is non-breachable these points must have motion if they contain energy (matter included)and at the very least are vibrating as long as a vacuum isn't space-less(which is impossible). Therefore as long as there is motion hyperspace can be almost continuous as the limit of the distance between each point approaches zero. Therefore it is possible that some paranormal phenomena may be right in front of us, between us and even inside us or inside solid objects and be difficult to detect if they are almost massless like photons or any low energy electromagnetic radiation such as radio waves are.

If non-corporeal energy traverses hyperspace as it is discontinuous unless blurred or smeared, it is possible that thoughts as well as paranormal "phenomena "traverse hyperspace. As this might be true thoughts can be disseminated through space-time via hyperspace thereby traveling at velocities greater than "c" or $3x10^8$ meters/sec. If this is true thoughts have a pathway from the microtubules of the brain in all animal life throughout space-time to other microtubules explaining telepathy as well as K-suryon waves. Even "Spooky Action at a Distance may traverse through this medium. Paranormal phenomena may have their information trapped between the point of the discontinuous hyperspace. Generally things which are normally unexplainable might be explained.

CAN HYPERSPACE BE MATHEMATICALLY DETERMINED WITHIN SPACE-TIME?

Without digressing the Harmonic Spherical Bessel Functions can be applied to space-time in a decreasing diameter from infinity toward zero as a cone asymptotic to a spiral after the first event. Spherical Harmonics utilizing the Legendre Functions and Polynomials of a degree j and order m reveal the equation$(1-z^2)$ $d^2w/dz^2 - 2z\ dw/dz + [j(j+1) - m^2/1 - z^2]w = 0$ whereby j and m are complex numbers in format a+or – bi and a+bi=0 and a –bi=0. $j\ j(z) = (\pi/2z)^{1/2} \otimes J\ j + 1/2(z)$ *and h* $j(z) = (\pi/2z)^{1/2} \otimes N\ j + 1/2(z)$ *h* $j(1)(z) = (\pi/2z)^{1/2} \otimes Hj + 1/2(1)(z)$ *h2(z) =* $(\pi/2z)^{1/2} \otimes Hj + 1/2(2)(z)$. *Here and thenceforward* $\otimes$ *is dot product o or just listed without symbols.* As the wave function in the Schrodinger Equation incorporates ih or –ih spherical harmonics ties into space-time with regard to the wave function as indicated in the denominator of the Equation of Everything as + or – ih(Λ *ba* + ρ *ab*) *applying it to the toal energy density of matter.* Of course the compactification of string theory is a circle and this is a two dimensional representation of a sphere as a two dimensional hyper-surface being progressive shrunk from an infinite diameter to a point with infinite curvature as a cone asymptotoci to spiral space-time after the first event. Asymptotic expansion of the cylindrical(after time oscillation paradox forming the vortex) and spherical Bessel Function for

$|z|$ gives $Jm(z) = \sqrt{\dfrac{2}{\pi z \left[Am(z)\cos\left(z - \dfrac{m\pi}{2} - \dfrac{\pi}{4}\right) = Bm(z)\sin\left(z - \dfrac{m\pi}{2} - \dfrac{\pi}{4}\right)\right]}}$ *and*

$$Nm(z) = (2/\pi z)^\wedge 1/2[Am(z)\sin\left(z - \frac{m\pi}{2} - \frac{\pi}{4}\right) + Bm(z)\cos\left(z - \frac{m\pi}{2} - \frac{\pi}{4}\right)$$

with the| arg |z<π(arg is argument or maximum argument for z where |⊣|is the absolute value) in radians with respect to z and the expansion component of the spiral operator of space-time acting on angular momentum. The Spherical Bessel Functions relate to space-time as -1/2 e –i n cot theta whereby the Spherical Bessel Functions relate to j j(z)=(π/2z)^1/2 J + 1/2(z) *and h j(z) = (π/2z)1/2 N j + 1/2(z) h j(1)(z) = (π/2z) Hj + 1/2(1)(z) and finally h2(z) = (π/2z)^1/2H(2)j + 1/2(z)* where by d^2w/dz^2+2/z dw/dz)[1-j(j+1)/z^2]w=0 and j are integral values. ;This clearly shows that +or -1/2 e –i n cot theta where theta is z is e-i

n cos z/z $\sin z - \dfrac{\textit{where the z's or angles of trajectories as } \pi \textit{ radians cancel}}{z}$

. Utilizing these spherical Bessel Functions for h0(1)(z)=-e^iz/z and h-1(0)(z)=e^-iz/z one can derive the cotangent of the trajectory of the Big Bang as cos z/sin z where z=π *radians where j0 z = sin z ! j – 1(z) = cos z/z.* Here h0^(2)(z)=ie^-iz/z and h-1^(2)(z)= e^-iz/z such that j i(z)=z^i(-1/z d/dx)^I sin z/z and n i(z)=(-1)^i+1 j- 1-1(z) where j=(1,2,3,...). This leaves the n dimensional case of spiral space-time being acted upon as a Spherical Harmonic Bessel Function.

The Spherical Harmonic Bessel Function and the Cylindrical Bessel Function both describe space-time as the Spherical Harmonic Bessel Function describes spacetime as a whole and the Asymptotic Cylindrical Bessel Function describes spacetime curvature describing space-time as + or -1/2 e –incotangent z or theta in the quantum mechanics description of the equation of everything(see book The Equation of Everything). The Asymptotic Cylindrical Bessel Function describes hyperspace as it is discontinuous blurring or smearing into a continuous curve as per the path integral of *du/u* !! =ln u which describes spiral space-time which is a confluent of increasing or decreasing spheres as described by the Spherical Harmonic Bessel Function and the cylindrical effect is asymptotic to the corkscrew configuration of space-time as described by Albert Einstein in 1912. Combining the Spherical Harmonic Bessel Function and the Cylindrical(corkscrew configuration of space-time)Bessel Function produce the spiral configuration of space-time as the spherical harmonic function reduces or increases the diameter of the corkscrew or cylindric configuration of space-time.

CHAPTER FIFTEEN

THE BIG BOUNCE

Dr. Neil Turok as the Director of the Perimeter Institute of Canada and Dr. Steffen Gielen of the Royal Academy of Physics in London4 stated that with the laws of Quantum Mechanics predominating at Planck Time or 10^{-43} seconds there was a deceleration of the near infinitely dense quantum bubble resulting in a near complete reversal of the Big Bang accelerating the initial Big Bang back towards the center of the vortex of space-time prior to the main expansion of the Big Bang. This point has been debated by physicists since 1922 as there was a question with this initial Big Crunch as to whether or not it returned to a nearly infinitely dense quantum bubble. As this was PRIOR TO THE FORMATION OF HYDROGEN OR HELIUM the world of strings predominated. Using a new model for Conformal Symmetry in the quantum bubble there is extant mathematical proof in models purported by Dr. Steffen Gielen and Dr. Neil Turok. There are apparently new models supporting the idea of a Big Crunch before the Big Bang which was purported by this author in the book "What is the Dimension of Time?" as well as "Mega-physics, A New Look at the Universe". The concept of conformal symmetry would explain this author's 0,0 point which would be the fracture point in the center of the quantum bubble.

15.2 QUANTUM GRAVITY

In terms of the Equation of Everything using Planck Mass and the inertial mass R ab we get Curved Lorenzian or Riemannian Space-time as described by Weyl's Conformal Tensor is C

$$abcd(n)=2^{\wedge}n+1\frac{\pi\omega}{2^{n\pi\omega}}+2\pi(R\,abc+or-\frac{1}{2}R\,g\frac{ab}{\rho}ab \quad \text{where } i\hbar(\rho$$

$$+\Lambda\,ba)=R\,ab \text{ and } R\,ab=\sqrt{h\frac{c}{8\pi G}}\,.$$

The effect of gravity on Planck's Mass is R g ab which when coupled with the anti-gravity of Planck's mass is the reciprocal of Planck's Mass. It is therefore $(8\pi G/\hbar c)^{\wedge}1/2$ *as the square root in the numerator and denominator equals anything to the zero power or 1*

Therefore the gravity and antigravity effects by Planck's Mass cancel out as ~0 gravity whereby Weyl's Conformal Tensor or the curved Riemannian tensor for curved space-time=flat or Mintkowski Space-time as in the quantum bubble before the Big Bang. General Relativity is non-renormalizable with a negative n-dimensional gravitational coupling constant (k). The equivalence principle states that the laws of physics in a gravitational field are identical to those of a local accelerated frame of reference. This explains the relationship of inertial mass and gravity which is the curvature of space-time caused by inertial mass remain a constant regardless of any dimensional space discussed. In the string n-dimensional state space-time is curved in the same way by mass (even string sized) as when a black hole that is supermassive curves space-time as the event horizon is approached. For the equations of motion the power expanding the metric tensor encompassing the solution g(0) *μυ(the Lorenzian Metric) of the equations of motion we get the expression gμυ(x) = g(0)μυ + kh μυ where hμυ = graviton field and* $k=\sqrt{Gn}\,.$

In this case the Graviton Field is the action(s) of inertial mass indicated by R ab or the Ricci Tensor curving flat Minkowski Space-time into Lorenzian Curved Space-time in a conformal manner as described by Weyl's Conformal Tensor of gravity or C abcd.

The LeGrangian Action L 0 = 1/4[–($\partial \upsilon h \rho\sigma$)² + ($\partial \mu h \rho^\rho$)² – $2\partial\sigma$ $h\rho^{\rho\mu}h^{\sigma\mu}$ + $2\partial\rho$ $h\upsilon\sigma\partial$ $^\wedge\upsilon h^\wedge$ $\rho\sigma$ or ∂ $h^{\rho\sigma^\upsilon}$. The Legrangian or Le Grangian Action is the most likely action of the Lorenzian

Metric acting on the graviton field h with regards to μ and υ whereby μ relates to the mass curving space – time with υ relating to the velocity of motion of μ in the graviton field. The total action is the sum of the LeGrangian and gauge symmetry partition functions. L 0 = $-\frac{1}{2\partial}$ x $h\rho\sigma$ $V^{\rho\sigma\mu\nu\partial^\lambda}$ $h\mu\upsilon$ and V $\rho\sigma\mu\upsilon$ = $\frac{1}{2\delta}$ $\rho\nu\delta\sigma\upsilon$ $-\frac{1}{4\delta}$ $\rho\sigma\delta\mu\upsilon$ whereby V acts on a dual action tensor field with regards to the graviton field.

Inverting the matrix
V
$\rho\sigma\mu\upsilon$ reveals the Final Propagate. of the fourth degree covariant tensor. Quantum Gravity can be expressed in a formally non-renormalizable form as local symmetry leads to what are called Ward Identities which cancel divergent graphs of quantum or topologic loops. Note according to Ward Identities the higher loop counterterms can only exist if the theory is divergent or infinite. As the counterterms of quantum gravity are formally non-renormizable (as mentioned previously) the divergent quantum loops cancel as part of the Ward Identitites the way Bianchi's Identity works with fourth degree covariant and contra-variant tensor of Riemannian Space-time or Weyl's Conformal Space. Based on these arguments "Arg" quantum gravity is a finite or convergent theory. The normalization coefficient of the wave function in quantum mechanics is related to the probability of

the wave function of point particle "x" at time "t" existing in space along the boundaries of integration such that the coefficient of

$C = \int_{-\infty}^{\infty} \|(x,t)^{\wedge}2\| = 1$ or 100% probability distribution of the wave function of point particle x at time t is satisfied. Local symmetry groups relate to gauge symmetry in Yang Mills Theory and relates to non-Abelian subgrouping which are finite in nature and relate to Quantum Field Theory and therefore Quantum Gravity. Graviton fields must also follow local gauge symmetry in order to be non-divergent quantum loops and the probability of existence must be 100% in order to avoid "ghosts" or divergent functions. In this author's previous book "What is the Dimension of Time?" it was shown mathematically that trying to prove the existent of nothing reveals only mathematical "ghosts".

The final propagate
δ μρδνσ + δμσδρ – δμυδρσ ÷ k² + iε is the inversion of matrix V ρσμυ forming quantum gravity in the non-re-normalizable form. Here k=gravitational coupling constant i= $\sqrt{-1}$ and epsilon relates to the Gauss-Bonnet Identity as related to the total derivatives of the product of two anti-symmetric constant tensors whereby the topological invariant implies the square of the curvature tensors of space-time rather than the conventional meaning of a small metric approaching zero. The total number of loops that are quantum (topologic) loops that show relativistic invariance that describe 1-loop counter-terms are finite while the asymptotic or infinite counter-terms which are invariant cancel again with regard to higher quantum loops. {R^2μνρσ, Rμν^2, R^2} *are counterterms that are invariant whereby 1/R^2 describes space – time curvature of of the metric g μv. If* Tμv *or the stress energy tensor of the metric gμv = 0 then Rμυ –* $\frac{1}{2}$ *gμυR = 0*

Where R
μυ represents interial mass and gμν represents the metric curving space – time as the effect of gravity. ith regard to one finite quantum

loop the general relativistic va??? time is $R^{2\mu\nu\varrho\sigma}$. *In other words Einstein's Equation of Relativistic gravity with regard to motion is* finite (convergent) with regard to the 1 loop level.

The 2 loop level cannot be canceled by the equations of motion and C

$\mu\nu\alpha\beta$ *with regard to quantum gravity is less divergent and Weyl's Conformal Tensor* which comprise the Riemann Metric of space-time tensors whereby $1/\epsilon$ *reveals divergences which are eliminated by the Gauss – Bonnet Identity with regard to Quantum Field Theory.*

To conclude, quantum gravity in the lower loops tend to converge into the equivalent of a finite theory but there are still divergent systems associated with larger loops which do not all cancel with the Gauss-Bonnet Identity. In the lower loops the convergence might tend toward a limit of zero as an asymptote as the stress energy tensor in Einstein's Equation of Motion would tend toward zero in the above mentioned case. Infinite mass is a divergent value as total mass is finite albeit huge which would constrict space-time toward zero with infinite curvature without having space-time converge to zero as this to is an asymptote. The point is that absolute mass-less-ness will not be reached even prior to the formation of the quantum bubble or the bubbles of the multi-verse as the components of space had huge potential energy and miniscule kinetic energy separating the infinite number of parallel planes prior to the time oscillation paradox and that anti-gravity as dictated by the cosmologic constant was a factor in separating these planes or D-0-branes from forming the first dimensions prior to the time oscillation paradox. Zero gravity relates to mass-less-ness and does not occur.

Quantum anti-gravity from anti-matter strings self repelling cancel out virtually all of the quantum gravity in the quantum bubble and cause the unopposed expansion with the spring effect in the current of space-time from the center of the vortex toward a 0 acceleration point followed by a 180 degree reversal caused by the pull of space--time upon space-time back toward the center of the vortex. Of course this would mean that the weak force of Dark Energy caused by the Cosmologic Constant with antimatter repulsion would be almost exhausted when the spring is released the quantum gravity would actually exceed quantum anti-gravity as the directional moment would change by π *radians or* 180 *degrees. The mass of the quantum bubble is finite and expands in this univer???* to 10^64 kg. Naturally The Equation of Everything would say that space-time constricts considerably in the quantum bubble relative to space-time outside the quantum bubble like the center of a whirlpool of perfect fluid space-time but at Planck Time 10^-43 seconds space-time would be flattening from a near infinite curvature of the quantum bubble to curvature which approaches flatness from the Cosmologic Constant and Dark Energy prior to it's shifting it's direction by 180 degrees back toward the center. Of course based on this the time of expansion before the reversal back toward the center of the vortex is based on the magnitude of Dark Energy and it's pushing effect against conformal time and if the accelerated expansion of the galaxies slows toward zero and Heat Death this reversal may not have occurred yet after 13.7 billion years which would precede a Big Crunch when this universe spiral back toward the center of the vortex. It is also possible the reversal occurred less than a second after the Big Bang so the first second expansion of 6.75x10^34 erg could have been from matter-anti-matter annihilation and repulsion of anti-particles sequester in one pole of the bubble while matter sequestered at the opposite pole. Still this reversal did occur or will occur as Newton's Second Law, The Law of Conservation of Energy and a specific location in space-time for the Big Bang to occur would then be localized as well as the center of mass of our universe or conversely of the multi-verse. Finally the formation of the multi-verse can also be postulated in an analogous way as our universe except one quantum bubble would become a 700 googlplex or more quantum bubbles or manifolds of different configurations such as Calabi_-Yau Manifolds and myriad other configurations and in this case the bubble for our universe would follow a Big Crunch of another universe (as previously mentioned).

In a sense Quantum Gravity would tend to be convergent as space-time curves inward with gravity (curvature inward of space-time caused by mass) and Quantum Anti-gravity would be reciprocal curvature of the flattening of space-time caused by strange or hybrid mass and might be considered divergent as space-time is curved outward. THIS DOES NOT MEAN THAT DIVERGENT HIGHER LOOPS NOT CANCELLED BY THE GAUSS-BONNET IDENTITIES WOULD BE RELATED TO ANTI-GRAVITY AS QUANTUM GRAVITY AND ANTI-GRAVITY ARE OPPSOITE SIDES OF THE SAME COIN; THE WAY SPACE-TIME CURVES. Every question regarding "The Big Bang' calling it a singularity has now been answered. THE LOCATION OF THE BIG BANG IS THE CENTER OF THE SPACE-TIME VORTEX CAUSED BY THE IME OSCILLATION PARADOX ACTING ON THE INFINITE NUMBER OF PARALLEL PLANES. BEFORE THE BIG BANG WAS NOT NOTHING SO THE LAW OF CONSERVATION OF ENERGY IS PRESERVED AS THERE WAS ALMOST INFINITE POTENTIAL ENERGY OF SPACE IN THE INFINITE PARALLEL PLANES WHICH CONVERTED TO KINETIC ENERGY AT THE TIME OSCILLATION PARADOX. NEWTON'S SECOND LAW HAS THE ACTION OF THE BIG BANG SPRING BACK TOWARD THE CENTER OF THE SPACE-TIME VORTEX AS THE EQUAL BUT OPPPOSITE REACTION. THE QUANTUM BUBBLE OR BUBBLES DEPENDING ON WHETHER THERE IS JUST ONE UNIVERSE OR A MULTI-VERSE DOESN'T EMCOMPASS EVERYTHING AS THE BIG BANG EX NIHILO STATES BECAUSE SPACE ISN'T NOTHING AND SPACE EXISTED PRIOR TO THE BIG BANG. NOTHING IS WITHOUT ANY PROPERTIES AND IS SPACE-LESS, MASS-LESS

AND WITHOUT ENERGY EITHER POTENTIAL OR KINETIC. ALSO NOTHING ALWAYS WAS AND WILL ALWAYS BE NOTHING AND NOTHING CANNOT BECOME SOMETHING WITHOUT A CATALYST AND THE CATALYST IS THE ROGUE TACHYON DROPPING TO THE SPEED OF LIGHT TRIGGERING THE TIME OSCILLATION PARADOX AND TACHYONS ARE SOMETHING AS IS SPACE. THEREFORE NOTHING DOESN'T EXIST.

RELATIVITY WITH REGARD TO THE MASS DENSITY OF THIS HOMOGENEOUS ISOTROPIC UNIVERSE AND THE BIG BANG

The present mass density of the background microwave radiation at the present is 1-^-3 or 1/1000 th of the mass density of matter. The B.M.R. should have been a dominant contribution to the mass density of this universe. As a→ 0 *the temperature in degrees kelvin approach ten million degrees. At this point the Hubble* Acceleration factor approaches zero before The Big Bang.

$a(\tau) = \dfrac{\frac{4c^1}{4}\tau^1}{2}$ *where rho* $\rho = \dfrac{3}{32\pi G\tau^2}$ *and* ρ *is the mass density of the universe. Again to simplify* $a(\tau) = \sqrt{\tau(4c)}^1 / 4$. *The mass density* $\rho =$

$n \sum_1^n \alpha i \; gi \; \dfrac{\pi^2}{30} h^{3c^5}$ $(KT)^4$ *where T is the absolute temperature* $K = space - time$ *curvature.* $\alpha i \to \dfrac{7}{8}$ *for ferminons and 1 for bosons with n being the number of states or eigenstates of radiatio???*

With g i=spin degeneration factor and τ = *time, Hubble Time or Conformal Time.*

If the mass density, KT it acts like zero mass due to 0 space-time curvature which comprises vacuum space comprised of leptons and gluons which are essentially massless with near infinite potential energy. $t\acute{e}\,\dfrac{a}{a'} = 2\tau$ *so as the mass density* =

$\sum_1^n aigi\left(\dfrac{\pi^2}{30}h^{3c^5}\right)KT^4$ *so in the denominator of The Equation of Everything the* $(KT)^4 \pi(\pi) \div 30\hbar^3c^5)KT^4$ *as the sum of* $\alpha\,i\,g$

i is the mass density of this universe. Becomes zero because the space-time curvature in a near vacuum state or Fermionic State approaches zero so if K~0 then KT~0 and KT)^4 ~0 so R ¡ *abcd* (0,1) → *infinity in the 0 and first eigenstate.* $2\pi(R$ *abc + or* $- \frac{1}{2}R$ *gab/ih(Λ ba + ρ ab) have Λ ba + ρ ab = the mass density $(KT)^4$ where K → 0 so in the o eigenstate pre Big Bang and pre – First Event space space was clearly infinite and time was infinitely dilated or in essence stop???*

In the Infinite Parallel Plates there was zero curvature as in the Fermionic or Vacuum State. Also the temperature in degrees kelvin would be negligible so the denominator would still approach zero and the numerator would become space-time=space with almost zero gravity and anti-gravity due to the negligible mass of space from leptons and gluons. In other words space-time=space→ ∞.

CHAPTER SIXTEEN

THE PROPERTIES OF ELECTROMAGNETIC RADIATION AS MATTER

According to Albert Einstein light is bent by gravity. This can only ne possible if photons have mass. It has been scientifically determined that the mass of a photon is not zero albeit miniscule. 1 At or about absolute zero photons have been slowed down in the laboratory to 36 miles per hour 2;this deceleration cannot occur unless photons have a measurable mass. Because photons have a measurable mass they can be considered matter as the equivalent mass from the de Broglie Equation $\lambda = h\dfrac{}{mc}$ where λ is the deBroglie Wavelength.. Based on this equation and using the Boltzmann Equation one can prove that electromagnetic radiation occupies the gaseous state of matter and the plasma state of matter depending on the environmental temperature. Also one can demonstrate that in black holes radiation occupies all states of matter including liquid, solid, and Boso-Einsteinian condensate.

Once shown that radiation is gaseous one can apply Boyle's Law and Charles' Law eo illustrate that as a perfect gas it follows the properties of any gas at standard temperatures and pressure (STP). Then one can apply the Perfect Fluid Equation for space-time with radiation as a perfect gas to attempt to predict radiation behavior in different media at super high pressures or at temperature extremes. vrbo.com

BACKGROUND

THE BOLTZMANN EQUATION *describes a fluid transport equation not in equilibrium according to statistical mechanics. The entropy of a given state S=k LnW where k=Boltzman constant1.38062 x10 -23 joules/degrees kelvin and W is the number of microstates of the system. It represents the number of ways molecules in a thermodynamic system can be arranged.4. Considering the Perfect Fluid Equation for space-time manifolds and photons of electromagnetic radiation in the form of a PERFECT GAS, ONE CAN USE AVOGARDO'S NUMBER 6.023X10 23 MOLECULES/MOLE OF AN IDEAL GAS AT STANDARD TEMPERATURE AND PRESSURE in the statistical mechanics of the Boltzmann Equation over six dimensional space-time to determine the entropy of a macro-state involving an ideal gas(electromagnetic radiation)in the microstates of the system W and then compare it with Steven Hawking's figure for black hole entropy of 0.29 in which 252 separate states of matter exist according to S=N $\sqrt{}$ Q1Q5 where N is the number of states Q1 and Q 5 are the charge differentials of the states in a black hole or Q1=one brane and Q5 is a 5 brane. N should approximately equal W in the Boltzmann Equation as the number of microstates of the macro system. Statistical thermodynamics reveals that the number of microstates corresponding to each photon is W where W=N!/ΠiNi! WHERE Ni= the microscopic condition of position and momentum (p). Given electromagnetic radiation as an ideal gas of N photons the probability of each state is equal to ||W||2 or W=N!/ΠiNi! The force and diffusion theorem the derivative of f = total change of collisions according to the Lionville Theorem and Hamilton's sequations of colli???*

Df/dt where d is the partial derivative of the total change with regard to time with respect to collisions Δtd33rd3p = Δfd3rd3p where $F(r + \frac{p}{m}t, p + f \Delta t$ A and $t + \Delta t$ are the derivatives of N the number of collisions equaling Δf d3rd3p where d 3 is three dime???

Total phase space. THE COLLISION LOSS AS A FORCE FIELD ACTING ON PHOTONS IN SPACETIME AS A PERFECT FLUID+F(R, T) WHERE M=MASS OF THE PHOTONS OR 10-23 grams giving the partial derivative of f with regard to time + p/mΔf + F the partial derivative of f with regard to p(momentum) = the partial derivative of f with regard to t with respect to collisions and if no collisions occur Between photons you get the Liouville Equation which is the collision loss of photons in phase space acting on t where t=time.

THE PERFECDT FLUID EQUATION IS THE RATIO OF PRESSURE (P) TO ITS ENERGY DENSITY ρ WHERE $W = \frac{P}{\rho}$. POISSONS EQUATION STATES THAT THE DERIVATIVE OPERATOR OF A DUAL VECTOR FIEL??? $4\pi\rho$ AND THE COMBINED GAS CONSTANT IS. 0821 WHERE $\rho MRT = \rho Mc2$. C = the thermal speed of molecules $= \sqrt{\ }$ RT where T = degrees kelvin for a perfect gas and $w = \frac{p}{\rho} = \frac{pC2}{pc2}$ where C = c therefore $a\frac{c}{c} = 1$ w $\frac{p}{\rho}$ for a cold gas of electromagnetic radiation or the $\frac{pressure}{t}$ heenergy density of matter or radiation of matter is unity for W in other word $\rho = p$ the energy density of matter equals the pressure of an ideal gas. The energy density of matter of electromagnetic radiation as determined by frequency (v equal its pressure the phase space with regard to time of spacetime in the perfect fluid equation Q.E.D.

Laser Technology involves a matrix whereby photons are trapped in a gaseous, liquid or solid matrix. In a sense lasers are light amplification in a gaseous or liquid suspension and can be used as a catalyst in trapping as little as a pictogram of photons in an environment similar to the super pressures of a black hole as a new energy source or fuel. Laser stands for light amplification by stimulated emission of radiation. Optical amplification through stimulated emission of electromagnetic radiation is how a laser emits light columnated overlarge distances with coherence.. A gain medium is excited by a source and a gain medium adsorbs energy to be trapped between two resonators. A photon of radiation repeats in the gain medium and is emitted through an aperture.

Boltzmann's H Theorem

H is the probability integral over what is known as velocity space. H is the quantitiy of events or metrics fpr N statistically independent particles. With v=velocity in d3 space $H=\int P(\ln P) d3\, v = <\ln p>$ *or the expectation value of the natural log of the probability of N particles moving at velocity S = entropy = –NkH where k = the Boltzmann constant. For electromagnetic radiation v = c and P approaches but doesn't reach 1. Therefore as* $\ln 1 = 0$ *H* $= \int p(\ln P)d3v = 0$ *As s = –NkH and H = 0 the entropy of this system for a black hole approaches zero. So according to the H theorem*

N particles moving at v=c in a black hole or the quantum bubble pre 'Big Bang" has a statistical probability of 100% for interaction of events or metrics with approaching zero entropy. In a black hole entropy is postulated by Steven Hawking as 0.29 and approaches the statistical conditions reached by the Boltzmann H Theorem. Motion between photons is dampened to the degree that a liquid solid and Boso-Einsteinian condensate phase of matter can be reached.

CHAPTER SEVENTEEN

THE MASS OF ANTI-PARTICLES AND THEIR PROPERTIES

This article is a detailed description of the mathematical exposition describing the properties of antimatter including a variable mass. It will also delve into practical applications of matter -antimatter systems as a potential energy source and the risks involved with an unsecured system. Antiparticles have been experimentally determined in CERN, Switzerland to have a positive mass. According to Newton's Law of Gravitation Force of gravity=G m1m2/r 2 or the force of gravity equals the gravitational constant G times the product of two masses divided by the distance between the masses squared. To get a negative gravitational force or antigravity would require one of the two masses be a negative mass. As matter and antimatter annihilate that would cause a modest repulsion between matter and anti-matter. As matter and antimatter attract it is unlikely that antimatter has a negative mass. However, using math the Force of gravity can also be negative if the mass of two particles is as such mass/i mass2/i so the radius squared becomes a -1(radius) squared. A mass for antiparticles could be and has been mathematically proven as the mass of ordinary matter/i or the square root of -1,This mass is a hybrid between positive mass and negative mass and oscillates during and throughout the distance from the positive non- oscillating mass. This oscillation of the mass coupled with the collision with positive mass triggers the annihilation reaction between antiparticles and particle yet it would still register as positive mass when weighed but would qualify as strange matter having the strange property of oscillating hybrid mass between negative and positive.

BACKGROUND

This author is able to mathematically prove using the Harmonic Oscillator that antimatter has a variable mass which is why after annihilation with matter strange matter in the form of quarks and gluons result. Particles and antiparticles have the same quantum number but opposite charge and quantum spin. Matter anti-matter annihilation result in the production of gamma rays, force carrier particles such as gluons and a W/Z force carrier particle. Positron and electron annihilation result in gamma rays with a rest energy of .511 Mega electron volts1; however protons and antiprotons result in mesons which can decay into neutrinos, positrons electrons and more gamma rays.

Physicists at the Brookhaven Laboratory have determined the existence and detected strange quarks in antimatter nuclei. The Relativistic Heavy Ion Collider(RHIC) detected an anti hyper-triton 2 which has an antiproton, antineutron and anti-lambda particle. The anti lambda particle is an extremely heavy antinucleus and is produced when gold ions are collided at very high energies producing quarks, antiquarks, and gluons which when cooled produce hyperons, up quarks and down quarks. These subatomic particles are all classified as hadrons

Particles produced by these collisions produce particles below the N-Z plane produced by nuclei; N being the number of protons, N the number of neutrons and S the degree of strangeness of the subatomic particle. Evaluation of strange quarks which are or=proposed to be in the collapsed neutron stars which are pre-black hole can determine what happened at or about Planck Time 10-43 seconds at 'The Big Bang" when a plasma soup of quarks was formed including up-quarks, down-quarks, and strange quarks.

MATHEMATICAL EXPOSITION

Mathematically the Harmonic Oscillator can fluctuate between 0 degrees or 0 radians and 180 degrees or π radians where the sine of these extremes is 0 and the sine of the extremes of π and 2π radia???

Is also 0 but from a mirror image deflection of the energy state being measured or operated on with regard to time. The Hamiltonian operator $\mathcal{H}=$p 2/2m+kx 2 and the Energy of the system $=(n+1/2)\omega$ where ω is the angular velocity n = the quantum level of the system p = momentum indicator which = mass times velocity k = the spring constant and x is the period displacement.

In an oscillating antimatter mass p=1/2(mω)1/2(r+r') where r has canonal commutation [p, x] and the Hamiltonian operator $\mathcal{H}$=1/2ω(rr'+r'r). For positive mass p=1/2(m$\sqrt{m\omega}$ (r + r')cosθ where θ = o degrees or o radians. For negative mass. p = $\sqrt{2m\omega}$ (r + r')cosθ where θ = π radians or $\sqrt{2m\omega}$ (r+r')cos θ where θ = π radians

P=momentum
ω = angular velocity and the x coordinate along with x' will be the complex conjugate of p amd p'.

X=i(2mω) $\frac{1}{2}$ – (r – r')cosθ for positive mass x = i(2mω) – 1/2 cos θ and for negative mass x' = i(2mω) – $\frac{1}{2}$ – (r – r') cosθ – where θ=o radians for positive mass and π radians for negative mass. cos 0 = 1 cosπ = –1 so it follows that $p = \dfrac{\frac{1}{2(m\omega)1}}{2(r+r')times}$–1 or $p = \dfrac{m\omega 2}{2(r+r')1}$ and $p' = \dfrac{m\omega 2}{2(r+r')}$ –1 The complex conjugates x and x' are i(2mω) – 1/2

97

cos $o(r - r')$ and $x' = i(2m\omega) - \frac{1}{2} cos\pi(r - r')$ -1/2=1/square root of mass x angular velocity+or-1 (r-r')I NOTE; cos θ *is in the numerator for* $o \leq \theta \leq \pi$ *and* r = *radius of rotation*

That is if $(2m\omega)$ *to the plus and minus one half power respectively or their sqaure roots.*

The zero point energy equation 3 is the Hamiltonian 2 Operator H = $\int_0^\pi d\sigma$ *(PuXu) – L where Xu has .. above.* L=p uX u-1/2 e(p2u + m 2 as the first order form of the Hamiltonian operator at ther zero point energy. σ *relates to the equations of motion + τ to – τ where τ relates to relative time.* Also, using Poisson's Equation $\nabla 2=4\pi\rho$ *for a dual vector field* (r, r') *oscillating between;=$4\pi\rho cos\theta=4\pi\rho(+1)$ and $4\pi\rho(-1)$ or $4\pi\rho$ and $4\pi - \rho$ in the dual vector field revealing + and – energy density of mass.* The dual vector field is (r, r') for =ρ and (r',r) for $-\rho$. In the zero point energy phase or using the massless null vector, an Abelian anti -symmetric tensor field can give a super-space formulation using tensor gauge theory with a massless Abelian anti -symmetric tensor field of rank 2. The stress energy tensor T ab can in oscillating mass(which nets out as zero mass between =1 and -1)can be shown as anti commutative as T ab=T ba nd T ab=-T ba such that T ba=-T ba,–T ab=T ba,-T ab=T ba and T ba=-T baas T ab cos0=T ab T ab cos π=-T ab T ab cos π=T ba, T ba cosπ =-T ab. In the zero point energy state the stress energy tensors are Abelian and anti -commutative.3

CONCLUSION

The momenta and coordinates of the oscillating mass represented by the complex conjugates p, x of the oscillating mass nets zero in the zero point energy stage.

PRACTICAL APPLICATIONS:

At .511 mega electron- volts from collisions matter anti-matter annihilation could possibly be a superior energy source to nuclear power if and only if containment of gamma rays will render it safe. The cost of such traps and screen may also be prohibitive and while plants may be strategically located in thinly populated areas and the energy transmitted to quadrants of various countries can an accident be avoided? In medicine positrons are used now in nuclear imaging of metastatic sites called PET scans, Positron Emission Tomography which help determine whether or not treatments for metastatic carcinomas are effective or not. The mechanism of action of the PET scan involves injection of the isotope Flu-deoxy-glucose(18 F)which is also known as FDG which is chemically mixed with radioactive isotope fluorine-18 substituted for a hydroxyl group in glucose as a positron –emitting radioactive isotope. A PET scanner can detect FDG in its distribution throughout the body. The 18F-FDG is taken up by the brain, kidney and malignant cells where phosphorylation stops glucose release preventing further metabolism so the molecule undergoes further radioactive decay while in the cell. Finally the 2'-flourine group is converted to 18 O-;which is heavy oxygen, which can be excreted normally.4As fuel the price of converting antimatter into high energy matter would be prohibitive albeit extremely efficient if enough antiparticles could be gleaned for use as a fuel.

G.R. Schmidt, H.P. Gerrish and J.J. Martin at the NASA Marshall Space Flight Center in Huntsville, Alabama have proposed Antimatter production for propulsion applications.. They propose anti-protons as a catalyst in fission based thrust production. The energy cost of 1 microgram can be affordable at 6 million dollars and can be used for spaceflights and intra-stellar space missions based on antimatter catalyzed fusion.5.

This article by the above delves into six alternative antimatter catalytic propulsion applications.

APPENDIX

The weak, strong and null energy conditions indicate that a positive mass rather than negative occurs in nature. Using path integrals with a flow-line integral over curve C for the null vector and using the stress energy tensor T ab the path integral $c =$ *T ab kakb d* $\times \geqq 0$ *where a and b are superscripts of k and k is the null vector.. The weak energy condition state* that for each time a vector field is observed non-negative density of matter is perceived. The above uses Poisson's Equation which states that the derivative operator of a dual vector field equals $4\pi\rho$ *where* ρ *is the energy density of matter.* $\rho = T$ *ab x n xb* ≥ 0 *and n and b are superscripts to x. Every future point vector field – T b a y b where a and b are superscripts in the tensor equation must be future point with reg???*

To times arrow, The strong energy condition has every future pointed vector field measures non-negative. T ab-1/2T g ab X a X b$\geq$ *o. again a and b are superscripts too x. Note: The Inflation Theory of Alan Guth and a scalar f???* Field with a positive potential violate this. [7] The Casimir Effect also violates the negative mass exclusion by matter. The Casimir Effect shows that $-\rho = \epsilon = -\dfrac{\pi 2}{720}$ $\dfrac{h}{d}$ 4 *where h = Planck's constant* ϵ *= energy density of matter and d* 4 *is* 4 dimensional spacetime. [6]

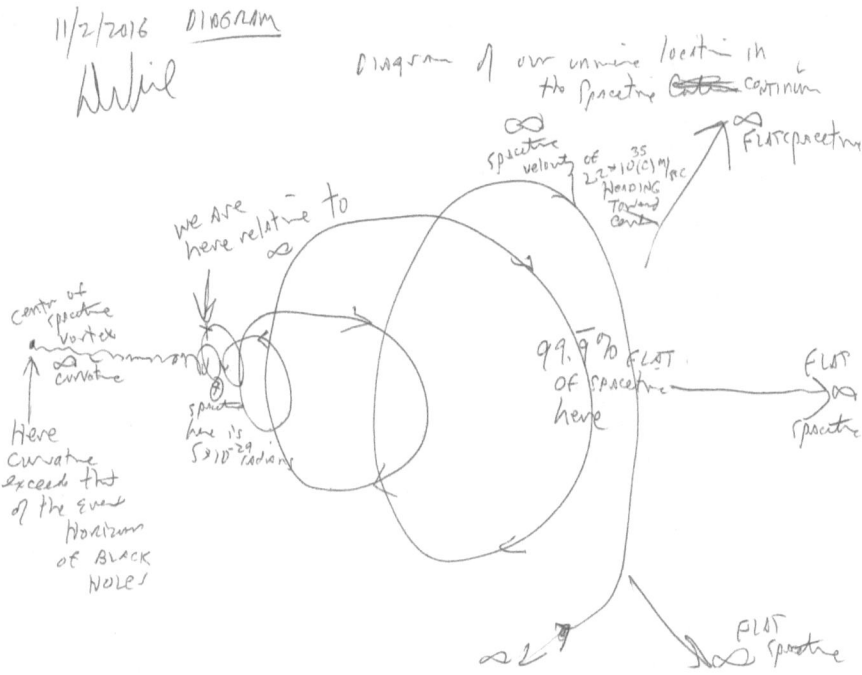

FOOTNOTES AND BIBLIOGRAPHY

1. Wikipedia. Annihilation, http:en.wikipedia.org/wiki/ Particle Annihilation 1.1 p.2
2. PHYSICS WORLD.COM RHIC Nets Strange Antimatter March 5, 2010.p.1 and 2
3. A Superspace Formulation of Abelian Anti-symmetric tensor gauge theory. Modern Physics Letters A 15(2000) p.965-978
4. Wikipedia. Fludooxyglucose (18F) Properties and Mechnism of Action. http:en.wikipedia.org/wiki/Fludooxyglucose
5. Antimatter Production for Near-term Propulsion Applications. Smith and Mayer Pennsylvania State University.
6. Wikipedia Energy condition. http:en.wikipedia.org/ wiki/Energy condition u
7. Guth, Alan. The Inflationary Universe.www.Edge.org

1. Kaku, Michio. Introduction to Superstrings and M Theory.1.8 p.37-38 Harmonic Oscillators Springer Press 1998.
2. ibid., see footnote 1
3. ibid see footnote 2
4. ibid see footnote 3
5. ibid see footnote 4.
6. ibid see footnote 5.
7. ibid see footnote 6
8. ibid see footnote 7

GLOSSARY AND DEFINITIONS

Abelian: an abelian group also known as a commutative group is the result of a group operation of 2 group elections which doesn't depend on their order. i.e., a set a, b combine to form another element a. b.()=operationof elements a and b. Anti-symmetric or Anti-commutative:- a= $a \leftrightarrow a = 0$. *Swapping the position of 2 arguments or elements negate the result.* $\sigma = group$ $\forall \alpha \epsilon \sigma$ Casimir effect: a small attractive force that acts between two parallel uncharged conducting plates or physical forces arising from a quantized field. Described as zero point energy of a quantized field in the intervening space between the objects

CHAPTER EIGHTEEN

BLACK HOLES AND RELATIONSHIP WITH DIFFERENT STATES OF MATTER AND BLACK HOLE ENTROPY

Matter and energy are entangled under some specific circumstances. Are strings flat matter which is 2 or possibly 1 dimensional or are they 0 dimensional as energy only with motions tension and vibrations as only frequencies. Is there a Law of Conservation of Matter as matter and energy are inter-changible and entangled under the extreme pressures and temperatures in a black hole? According the Schwarzchild Space-time there is a constriction of space-time with time dilating to almost infinity or in essence stopping at the Event Horizon of a Black Hole. Black holes emanate from collapsing matter in galaxies, neutron stars and possibly universes. As a consequence there should be a black hole at the 0,0 point which is the point of the "Big Bang" although in an isotropic universe scientists may not be able to locate it for a considerable period of time The initial rotational vectors in the expanding universe where rotation is progressively decreasing as space-time continues to push outward should be slightly measurable as the proximity to this 0,0 black hole is approached although iso-tropism generally precludes a center of gravity. Still it makes sense that the 0,0 point would be a center of rotation for the rotating and expanding universe(this universe in the multiverse) It is now postulated that all galaxies have a central black hole including the Milky Way and these galaxies rotate along the central axis of these black hole albeit at an extremely slow rate. If negative mass exists in a black hole it was mathematically determined in chapter of Schwarzchild Space-time that superimposition of region 3 on region 2 and regions 1 and 4 can cause the information to garner at the Event Horizon like a phonograph record or video tape. This relates to the idea of The Holographic Universe and translates everything into two dimensions. Regions 1 and 3 are left and regions 2 and 4 are cancelled. Region 3 has negative mass and superimposes on region Region 3 is reflected back on region2 with region 3 having a negative mass and region 2 having a positive mass and there canceling as per the math in chapter 5, leaving regions 1 and 4. This may be a solution to the Hawking Paradox which says that as a black hole evaporates information in the black hole is lost.

Regarding the 252 different states of matter within a black hole (Hawking) these would have to include all or most state under extreme pressure with significantly constricted space and extremely high density. If electromagnetic radiation including photons from light are absorbed into a black hole(making it invisible) would that radiation show matter or matter like characteristics such as the states of liquid radiation suspended in a condensate as in the experiment by Dr. Len Hau mentioned in the previous chapter. If radiation could occupy the different states of matter and if matter and radiation can be or are entangled then radiation can occupy a liquid and possibly a Boso -Einsteinian Condensate state at near 0 degrees kelvin. If this is true perhaps radiation can in the future be considered a "perfect gas" but again for that one would have to demonstrate mass in a photon although of course electrons and photons have mass as do anti-protons and positrons although the mass in the latter two may be considered "strange mass" which might be an oscillating hybrid between negative and positive mass although recorded as positive mass which may or may not have anti-gravitational effects rather than the effect of pure gravity.

In terms of The Equation of Everything" as space-time curves in manner reciprocal to ordinary space or curves inward when in the expanding universe space-time curves outward ¡ $n = R$ $abc - \frac{1}{2} R g \, ab \div R \, ab$ or ¡ $n = \Pi n = 1$ to $\infty \frac{1}{2^n \pi} g \, ab \, R \, abc - \frac{1}{2} R g$ $ab \infty \rho \, ab$ where the infinite product of $\frac{1}{2^n \pi}$ times the metric g ab times Mintkowski Space – time divided by the energy density of matter for the metric g ab reveals for a large mass

In constricting space reaches a point where $-1/2R \, g \, a \, b=R$ $a \, b$ where the space-time curvature variant of the mass R a b=inertial mass of the black hole such that ¡ $n = R \, abc \otimes 1$ where R abc constricts with near infinte curvature from R g ab and R ab is a huge number. The expression $\Pi \frac{1}{2^{n\pi}} \to \frac{1}{n\pi} g \, ab = \frac{1}{\infty} = 0$ space – time with near infinite curvature in a black hole with constricted space. Here ¡ $n \to 0$ as n approaches a large number. The expression ρ ab relates to R ab as the enrgy equivalent of the inertial mass R a b and incorporates the $1/c^2$ or $1/p^2 c2 + m^2 {}^\wedge c^4 =$ energy and p=momentum incorporates into ρ ab the energy density with regard to the metric g ab. Of course the $1/2 \pi$ relates to the spherical nature and circumference $2\pi\rho$ at the event horizon of a black hole w??? space-time is constricted down toward 0 with infinite curvature and as the areas where the energy density of matter ρ and inertial mass constrict more and more it goes from $\frac{1}{2\pi}$ to $\frac{1}{4\pi}$ to $\frac{1}{8\pi}$ times the metric g ab an stress energy T ab$\to 1$. as inertia $\leftarrow$ gravity. As ρ ab $\to$ large number the entire expression for ¡ $n \to 0$ but where does the energy go from the event horizon of a black hole. Answer quasars with Hawking Radiation being spumed out like a jet engine leaving the black hole cold as a $CO2$ cartridge would be cold after the contents of the cartridge were suddenly forced out. Therefore ρ ab would manifest the energy f *or the inertial mass R ab like a CO2 cartridge being discharge* over a protracted time period.

The expression S=2 $\pi(NQ1Q5)^{1/2}$ *describes black hole entropy in terms of it's 252 different disparate states.* This would be similar in some ways to $2\pi\rho$ = *circumference (space – time)* → 0 *so* ρ → 0 *deep within a black hole* and the diminishing sphere of space-time to a point is described by ¡ $n = \dfrac{1}{2^{n\pi} \, as} n \rightarrow \infty$ *gab*⊗*Rabc* – 0.5*Rg ab*⊗ρ *ab^* – 1 where space-time=$2\pi\rho$.

Note that a circle reducing to a point is a cone or asymptotically a spiral. Therefore the operator $\Pi n = 1$ *to* ∞ ½^$n\pi$ would be the spiral operator on space-time reducing it from a sphere to a point in a cone shape The Spiral operator would be $\Pi \dfrac{1}{2^n} \pi^1$ *where the infinite product Π is from n to ∞ eigen-states.*

The Bekenstein Hawking Equation for black hole entropy S=A/4Lp^2c^3A/4G$\hbar$ *where* $\hbar$ *= Planck's Constant* $6.63x10^{-34 joule}$ – sec *or* $meters^{2kg}$/*sec G = gravitational constant* $6.67x10^{-11}$ *newton meters/sec ^2 Lp = Planck length =* 10^ – 33cm *A=cross sectional area or kA/Lp^2 where k=Boltzman constant and Pl=$\hbar$— =* 10^{-33cm} *again. Black hole entropy (S) based on this is* $\dfrac{1}{4}$ *or also Steven Hawking postulated* 0.29. Black hole entropy is directly proportional to the area of the event horizon by the Boltzman Constant k which was explained earlier with the Boltzman Equation for different states of matter. This is the maximum entropy obtained by what's called the Berkenstein Bound and relates to the Holographic Universe and principle of a two dimensional fingerprint of information in the black hole at the event horizon. Supersymmetry was applied to black holes using D-branes and string theory duality with regard to the SO(32) string theory and the compactification of closed string theory IIa to a circle with regard to M theory.

The zeroth law states the surface gravity of the event horizon of a stationary black hole doesn't vary. The first law states that the the change in energy dE=k/8πdA + ΩdJ + ΦdQ where κ = surface gravity A = area of event horizon Ω = angular velocity J = angular momentum Φ = electrostatic potential of the charge Q The second law is that the horizon area is a non-decreasing function with regard to time or dA/dt> or =0. When it was discovered that Hawking Radiation was emitted by black holes and the area and mass (therefore gravity) decreased over time this was became a "weak law". The third law of black holes is that k or κ for surface gravity cannot be 0 The zeroth law states that surface gravity is similar to thermal equilibrium in thermodynamic systems in that a temperature doesn't vary neither does surface gravity κ in a black hole. Wikipedia; Bekenstein Entropy

In the equation $S(BH)=2\pi\sqrt{NQ1Q5}$ N is the number of states as mentioned before and Q1 relates to the one-brane which relates to effecting or carrying the electrical charge related to the monopole or the electron emanating from higher states of matter in terms of n-branes. Q5 relates to the charge relating to space-time as the electron has a cloud with a probability density that goes out to ∞ without reaching it but bounded by the event horizon of a a black hole.

Based on this $S=2\pi\sqrt{\ }$ (252) charge of an electron gas (space – time) Charge of an electron is 1.6x10^-19 coulombs and the 5 brane relates to near infinite curvature of a contracted area of space-time as told by $\frac{\Pi 1}{2n\pi}$ g ab R abc – $\frac{1}{2}$ r g ab ⊗ ρ ab^{-1} where n = number of eigenstates in n dimensional space. for the infinite product from n to ∞ giving spac???

½^nπ as $\frac{1}{2^0\pi}$ as space – time approaches the D – 0 state or D – 0 – branes making

$$\frac{1}{2\pi} = \frac{1}{2\left(\frac{22}{7}\right)} = \frac{7}{22(2)} = \frac{14}{22} \ so \ 44/7\sqrt{252(1.6x10^{-19})(\frac{14}{22})} = 6.14[(160.36)(1.6x10-19)]^1/2$$

which is 6.141(6x10-17=36.6x10^-17 as black hole entropy in the zero(0) dimensional state or the D-0-brane which is very close to 0 entropy while Steven Hawking postulated entropy of a black hole to be approximately 0.29. This is because while spacetime is constricted at the event horizon it still exists so there is no 0 dimensional state within a black hole which would make the 5-brane relate to a four or perhaps higher dimensional state with the 252 different states of matter including energy-matter conversion or entanglement due to the superhigh pressures and super cold temperatures. It is likely that Boso- Einsteinian Condensate would exist with a matrix that traps photons, electrons, positrons, neutrinos, anti-neutrinos, bosons and at near the zero dimensional state fermions. It is also possible that tachyons would be trapped in a black hole which would reverse time's arrow and have a negative mass or strange mass hybrid between negative and positive mass. It is these tachyons that would cause the –mass in the superimposed region 3 onto region 2 that would solve the Hawking Paradox. Whether radiation actually takes on a liquid state is agnostic but not impossible under those conditions.

If the spiral operator operates on the function R a b c-1/2Rgab⊗ $pab^\wedge$ – 1 and is inclusive of the metric g ab over the infinite product of eigenstates over n dimensional space it is asymptotic to Schwarzchild Space-time if the expression is reflected at the event horizon to express the increasing cone or spiral from approximately zero (0) dimensional space-time to n dimensional space-time where n goes from the D-0 eigenstate to D-n-eigenstate. This can be accomplished if Π *from n* = 11 *or n* = 10 *decends to n* = 0 *for the D – brane which gives an opening spiral or cone past the event horizon as there is a descending co???*

Cone at the event horizon with space-time spiraling in from ordinary space. The factor relating to the mass equivalent on both sides of the event horizon emanates from the function on which the operator is operating or "The Equation of Everything" so Schwarzchild spacetime$= \Pi n \dfrac{1}{2^{n\pi}} - \dfrac{\Pi n 1}{2^{n\pi} g}$ ab where the limits of the infinite product Π are from n to $\rightarrow D$ 11? and from D11 $\rightarrow$ n where n starts at $D = 1$ not $D = 0$ as the spiral is a modified cone acted upon by the metric g ab as per Rabc $- \dfrac{1}{2R} g$ ab Ä (ρ ab)^ – 1.

CHAPTER NINETEEN

DARK ENERGY AND DARK MATTER

It was questionable about whether dark energy and dark matter were related until the missing mass calculation for the mass equivalent of dark energy and the mass of dark matter were found to be congruous. As so they share charcaterisitcs and can be considered in the same gauge symmetry group. This can be negociated with the mechanism of the "Big Bang" which is like lighting a match. From a chemical standpoint (as previously mentioned) the unlit phosphors would be the homogeneous antimatter-matter mix, the Big Bang would be the light being struck, and the charred residual would be the dark matter while the energy expended would be the Dark Energy coupled with the energy from the annihilation of matter and antimatter in the "Big Bang".

As mentioned previously the antiparticle-antiparticle repulsion o\in the quantum bubble under extreme pressure and temperature force a huge anti-gravitation force to push matter with space-time outward after the rotational component of "The Big Bang" had almost completely slowed toward 0. The anti-gravitational force pushing galaxies apart from each other is Dark Energy and the residual antimatter that was burned out is dark matter. As the anti-gravitational moment of the interaction was carried off by the Dark Energy, Dark Matter has a gravitational effect instead of antigravity although it emanated from anti-matter.

As mentioned previously the particles of dark matter are on and about everything just as the BMR from the "Big Bang" is all pervasive, but the particles of dark matter are so small yet homogeneous that they might be a multiple of $Pl = h\dfrac{G}{c^3 or} 10^{-33} cm$ *which would make the density of this superfine powder or dust have a very sli???* slight measurable density in the massive volume of space although the gravitational effects from the mass are considerable although measured indirectly. This too was already mentioned.

It has been postulated that Dark Matter is composed of baryonic particles and neutrinos possibly with anti-neutrinos and anti-Hadrons as a residual from anti-matter and that Dark Matter acts as a type of "cosmic glue" which has been present since the "Big Bang"

There is a question as to how much of the cosmologic constant */\ is related to Dark Energy, but the force to push the 750 billion galaxies apart from each oth???* seems to be far greater than what was empirically measured for Dark Energy and greater than /\ *(the cosmologic constant) which relates to* $8\pi G/c^4$.

With a stretch of the imagination and some creative math one can see that the 1st, 3rd, 5th and all odd dimensions have dark matter sequestered as it's gravitational effect can only be indirectly measured and mass in the even dimensions 2nd, 4th, 6th, 8th etc. can have it's properties directly measured. This can evolve from the space-time formula of $-1/2e^{-i} n \cot$

θ *where* $\theta = \pi$ *radians which is the trajectory of the "Big Bang".* Odd powers of i give results containing I while even powers of I give real numbers such as $i^2 = -1$, $i^4 = -1$ etc while $i^1 = I$ and $i^3 = -I$ and

$i^5 = -I$ such that if this was the scenario due to the inert nature of dark matter its mass may be postulated mathematically mass of dark matter=mass of ordinary matter/i *or* $\sqrt{-1}$. This would be likely if dark matter which is anti-matter based showed anti-gravitational rather than gravitational effect as Fg=Gm1m2/r^2 where 6.67x10-11n-m/sec^2 or 10-11=G and m1=mass/i m2=mass2/i such that Fg=Gm1m2/i^2r^2=-1(G m1m2/r2) which would indicate mutual repulsion of antiparticles and anti-gravity. While it may be true that the odd dimensions may have dark matter and possibly most of the missing mass equivalent of Dark Energy forming the difference between what is measured and mathematically calculated as a prediction on we will still have to show strange or oscillating mass in dark matter (as burned out antimatter). This oscillating property would be between + and – mass and while experiments with the Hadron Collider in Cern, Switzerland are looking for anti-gravity between anti-particles and particle-anti-particle interaction before they annihilate, it has not clearly been demonstrated yet that anti-particles display pure anti-gravity although they do display some properties of anti-gravity. It also has not been demonstrated that anti-particles display anything except a positive mass. The question is this. How does experimentally show burned out antimatter in dark matter when it's effects can only be indirectly measured. Also is mass/i the same as strange or oscillating matter with a hybrid between +mass and –mass. If this property follows antimatter and antiparticles it may also follow dark matter with much huger antigravity with Dark Energy. Mathematically shadow odd dimensions cannot be ruled out but whether or not they contain the mass of dark matter or mass equivalent of dark energy is up to speculation.

CHAPTER TWENTY

THE SUPERBRANE

BY DR. MITCHELL ALBERT WICK

A SUPERBRANE is a membrane that encompasses everything and is so small that it encompasses all other membranes and all mass. Space-time can be subdivided down to 10^{-33} cm or Planck Length as the orbifold but below that the nature of space-time is up to speculation. It has been proposed by this author that space-time below Planck Length is formed by a confluence of quantum dots which have an approaching infinite curvature as a point would. These quantum dots vibrate and oscillate into each other making the "nothing space" between them approach zero as the frqency of vibration and oscillation exceed "c" or the speed of light 3×10^8 meters/second which further encompasses the idea that "nothing doesn't exist". It has been postulated by Einstein that the mass of every body exceeds that of 1000 suns. This would normally seem unlikely as space-time curvature in the universe is miniscule at 5×10^{-29} meters whereby most of the spiral curvature would be adjacent to the event horizons of black holes and whereby the majority of this universe is nearly empty space approximately 10^{22} km with a temperature of 2.74 degrees kelvin the BMR from The Big Bang. As 99.9999999999999999999% of the universe is empty space without mass or gravity (the curvature of space-time caused by mass) a vast majority of the universe is toally flat or 5X10^-29 meters of curvature which is asymptotic flatness. However most of the spacetime curvature is so closely adjacient to the mass of any and all particles including superstrings that it makes up the quiantum dot matrix where each dot has nearly infinite curvature and dots composed space-time on a level which is smaller than Planck Length. The summation of the curvature of each quantum dot relates directly to the space-time curvature metric of gravity or R g ab as in the action formula S=-1/2k^2(-g)^1/2R and develops an almost infinite number for the confluence of quantum dots which oscillate and vibrate at greater than "c" in essence *πc or the velocity of spacetime. These quantum dots are so miniscule that they could be 10^10*

Cm smaller than Planck Length and are therefore virtually unmeasurable with our level of technology but they would comprise the SUPERBRANE which is flexible and encompanies everything with every mass having internal motion which is greater than light speed in vibration and oscillation, The curvature of each component quantum dot approaches that of infinity as a quantum dot is asymptotic to a point and the sum of each quantum dots curvature added to the essentially flat space-time of virtually empty massless space would derive the line element equation or space-time curvature metric on Mintkowski flat space-time as in the equation of everything. And as a multitude of infinite curvature points in spacetime is reduced in size from essentially flat space-time the spiral operator used to measure space-time as the event horizon of a black hole can be utilized for all space approaching this massive superbrane.

So the equation ¡ *abcd* = Π *n* = 1 to $\infty \dfrac{1}{2^{\pi r}}$ *g ab Rabc* − $\frac{1}{2R}g\frac{ab}{\rho}ab$

where the infinite or near infinite number of dimensions that are so miniscule

That they dwarf Planck Length as in the subdivided on second of arc where each plane intersects with an infinite number of other planes as the curvature metric causes the planes to be nonparallel causing an infinite number of intersections or dimensions that are far smaller than Planck Length and incorporated in this MASSIVE SUPERBRANE WHICH EMCOMPASSES EVERYTHING AND HAS APPROACHING INFINITE space-time curvature to reflect the huge density of what apprears and is measured as a limited mass in small objects.

CHAPTER TWENTY-ONE

SPOOKY ACTION AT A DISTANCE

The phenomenon of "Spooky Action at a Distance" relates to the exchange of information such as electron spin over great distances which may change when an observer is present. This phenomenon with regard to electrons may be caused by an electron cloud which doesn't dissipate over great distances meaning the fingerprint or signature of the electron's information could exist kilometers away or farther distance which might not seem possible with normal physics. A similar phenomenon can occur with photon pairing although photonic information with the wave particle duality can travel at just under "c" if photons have a non-resting mass and "c" if photons are massless. The pairing of information between photons could be because the wave property of photons could be analogous to the electron cloud of an electron and since photons are virtually ageless and immutable, information is also immutable must be preserved and can be exchanged between paired photons over huge distances via the wave property of photon via De Broglie's Equation $\lambda = h\dfrac{}{mc}$ *where masslessness m = 0 makes an almost infinite wavelength and super high frequency with very high energy*

From the Planck's Equation
E(photon)=$\hbar v$ *where v = frequency. Based on these equations very low frequency waves or photons such as radio wave??? have*

more of a mass than high frequency waves such as x or gamma rays. Massive objects also have a corresponding wavelength regardless of the velocity of the massive object ($\lambda = h\dfrac{}{mv}$ and *the wavelength gets shorter as the velocity* ® *c.* The observed positions of electrons was not where they were supposed to be due to electron cloud probability distributions of $|.e\ E| > \pi m^2/$ ln 2 where e=electric charge (Q) and E- electric field and mass is electron mass and probability of a generator penetrating a sphere of diameter of z such that $|z|$ leads to an asymptotic divergence of probability with a continuity limit of varying field strength and the definition of probability being violated by the tail of the distribution. With regard to carrier densities, the density distribution of matter is gc(E)=$8\,\pi\sqrt{\dfrac{2}{h^3}\dfrac{me^3}{2}}$ *where ℏ = Planck's constant and* $\sqrt{E-Ec}$ *for E > Ec has Ec as the conduction on ba???* between the density of energy states and is where r=0 on the sphere upon which the generating function acts where 2r=z. In this instance "g" is the scalar metric not G. Discrete levels of Normalization for electrons in the volume of an infinite diameter sphere can be summated into a convergent system where the field strength and asymptotic behavior of the probability distribution acts on all particle masses with carrier densities as the infinite diameter of the sphere is forced to converge at the circumference or $\pi|z|^2$ *where z = diameter and* $|z|^2$ *is the probability distribution.* $\Sigma z=0$ to $z \to \infty\left(\dfrac{4}{3\pi r^3}\right)h(E-Ec)$ where the volume of the sphere is $4/3\pi r^3$ *and z is the diameter with the infinite sum of the system.*

Based on the wave function with Schrodinger's Equation the probability distribution of the electron field density with regard to the charge of an electron will diverge to ∞ *as* $z \to \infty$ *until the volume is such that z converges with the circumference which must be at time =* ∞ *according to relativity as the circumference is expanding faster than the diameter(z).*

As the electron cloud distributions of many or all electrons in a field which can stretch out vast distances information on spin can be exchanged between electrons in the electron gasses that compose the field.

The Schrodinger Equation $\psi(E) = gc(E) =$

$$\frac{8\pi\left(\dfrac{2me^3}{h^3}\right)^1}{2}\sqrt{E - Ec\int_{Ec}^{\infty} gc(E)F(E)dE}$$

Where n= carrier density f(E)=Fermi Dirac Proabability Function

and n0$= \displaystyle\int_{Ec}^{\infty}\dfrac{8\pi\left(\frac{2}{h^3}\right)^1}{2}$ $or\,8\pi\sqrt{2/h^{\wedge}3}$ $me^{\wedge}3/2\sqrt{Ev - E^1 + ef}$ E/kT

dE where k=Boltzmann constant exists for each specific state of an electron gas. The action(S) of the metric g for an electron with a carrier density of E v acting on the electron gas has a 100% probability with localization of the electron gas at infinite diameter z in the expanding sphere of space-time. The action

$S = c^{\wedge}8/12\dfrac{\pi GR1R2(-EvE)^3}{2r}$ *where R1 = p0 and R2 = n0 and P0*

is the probability of the carrier density of E v as a state of matter = ρ0. With R1 as carrier density of state of matter acting on n0 of the electron the action

Of the carrier density n has a probability of 100 % for the electron gas acting on *p the energy density of all states of matter as determined by the Boltzman Equation where* K=Boltzman constant and T=temperature in degrees kelvin. Therefore there is a 100% probability that the carrier density of an electron gas will interact with the density of matter in a diameter(z) traveling an infinite volume and not converging with the circumference until the diameter and the circumference meet which is why electron gas paths must intersect and exchange information such as spin.

With regard to photons which are purported to be massless and traveling at "c" while electrons travel at approximately v=0.65 c photon pairing is much simpler to explain in terms of contracted space and dilated time. Information of a photon (as dictated by the energy level=$\hbar v$) *travels vast distances at "c"* and the information may actually also change with or without an observer assuming that the temperature is 2.74 degrees kelvin or higher. To travel faster than this the photon would have to be a wave or electromagnetic radiation rather than a particle bending or warping contracted space to transmit the information. Photons and waves are supposed to travel in a double helix path burrowing spirals into space rather than in a strictly straight line (if photons were actually massless) Despite this the "Spooky Action(S) at a Distance" is still quite spooky and resembles the technique for a transporter device.

CONCLUDING REMARKS

The purpose of this book is to introduce to the scientific community mathematical adaptations of concepts regarding the five duel string theories and M Theory in terms of "The Equation of Everything" and applying this equation to Black Holes with the Spiral Operator to demonstrate it's congruence to Schwarzchild Spacetime. In addition this author has attempted to solve the "Hawking Paradox" using superimposed regions of Schwarzchild Space-time with negative mass from tachyons (replacing + mass bosons) to net out the information over dilated time as 0 so information isn't lost in a Black Hole. Also, the existence of Dark Matter has perplexed physicists for 25 years and in this work this author has attempted a new theory based on math that Dark Matter exists on everything as a fine microscopic powder with significant mass but in the volume of the universe has no measurable density making it invisible. In addition there was a purported mechanism that when anti-matter and matter either blew out with "The Big Bang" at the 0,0 point and inflated out with Inflation. Again consider light a match with the light being the Big Bang, the residue on the top of the match is Dark Matter, the force of anti-gravitational (push) is Dark Energy and the phosphors of the unlit match is the anti-matter matter mix. The residual matter after the anti-antimatter repulsion and anti-matter matter annihilation is the dark matter and ordinary matter after "The Big Bang".

The fact that string theory can be compactified (curled up) into a circle as IIa string theory and possibly M Theory lead one to realize that the equation of arc length s=rθ *can relate to spacetime and the Riemann Forces such that space – time accelerates and the Riemann forces curve spacetime as increments of θ from 2π radians*

$2n\pi$ *radians where the circumference of the circle (compactified IIa closed string theory and M ???* theory outruns the diameter of the circle which represent the Riemann metric in both directions with ¡ *ab* = ¡ ^*ab* such that the radius is the + or – Riemann metric. In this case as the circumference of space-time is *$2\pi R$ and since 2R = d then the rate at which space – time is "outrunning"* the Riemann forces is *πc as space – time and perhaps tachyons are the only quantities that can exceed the speed of light boundary*

CHAPTER TWENTY-TWO

IS THIS UNIVERSE TWO DIMENSIONAL?

Flat matter consists of photons, strings(open and closed) and anything else perceived as a holographic projection. The 2 dimensional lattice equation of Michio Kaku indicates a relationshipship between quantum mechanics and relativity with regard to the critical exponent when everything comes apart. Could this relate to"The Big Bang" or "Big Crunch'?

The curling up or compctification of string theory or M Theory is a circle not a sphere and the dimensions which are greater than two in a holographic construct of the world sheet are compactified dimensions and string sized forming membranes. White noise utilizing CMB data contains trillions of bits of information which are string sized 10^{-33} cm or smaller In this author's first book "Megaphysics, A New Look at the Universe"(2003)it was postulated that a two dimensional universe would exist as would a world sheet in string theory helping to unify quantum mechanics and relativity. This would include space in dilated time comprised of almost massless photons of electromagnetic radiation which would travel at all speeds except zero depending on the medium they pass through and because influenced by gravity such as in black holes they do have miniscule mass as does space. So in essence the vacuum or fermionic state of matter may be comprised of photons with gluons holding space together, while tachyons still exist above the velocity of photons traveling backwards in time which would be infinitely slow if time were totally dilated. The event horizon or any active black hole contains bits of information which would or might appear to the observer as being two dimensional as well as in dilated time and photons are postulated to have existed virtually always. In addition strings whether open or closed are comprised of flat matter or energy which is also flat matter and therefore two dimensional The critical exponent of the 2D lattice equation may relate to the Big Bang w ith reference to criticality as might a Big Crunch.

'The Holographic Universe 'by Dr. Micheal Talbot indicates that two dimensional projections would exist in terms of the World Sheet as purported by string theory as strings are two dimensional. Paranormal phenomena like "ghost sitings" could be two dimensional images on a background three dimensional plane as "ghosys" are indicated as "white noise" or in the low energy fradio wave band as electromagnetic raidiation mwhich is comprised of photons which are flat matter or two dimensional.

A supposedly absurd theory purported that our universe is a computer program supported by physicisits like Dr. Neil deGrasse Tyson of the Hayden Planetarium may seem absurd but if this uniberse is comprised of flat matter which has two macroscopic dimensions and a near infinite number of string sized dimensions which comprise a super-brane or supermembrane as purported in M Theory then this would be compatible with a computer program comprised of a multi-googlplex of bits of data or information forming the program. This is compatible with the dolution to the Hawking Paradox which shows that the bits of information at the evetnt horizon of any active black hole is dispersed or dissolved in space-time as a diffusive process such as a suspension where the bits are so miniscule that they can't be detected by any present technology. What would control the program though?The Higgs Field comprised of tachyons and the massive Higgs Boson and how would the "computer" be turned on and off? Is the Big Bang where a rogue tachyon drops to the speed of light causing a a time oscillation paradox and the vortex of space-time from an infinite number of parallel planes be the turning on by the deterministic rogue tachyon dropping from above light speed to the speed of light causing the time oscillation paradox. And would a Big Crunch be the turning off of the computer program? Many of these ideas would br very difficult to prove but new evidence just released. On the Jpurnal of Physics Review Letters there is evidence that a two dimensional matrix exists with googolplex of microdata which this author believes forms a super-BRANE. It solves problem's with Einstein's Theory of Gravvity as in the two dimensional state the curvature of space-time caused by mass reaches as asymptototic limit approaching zero without reaching it in the two macroscopic dimensions while the superBrane emcompasses the other infinite dimensions. This two dimensional world sheet helps to unify quantum mechanics and trlativity and while the "Computer Program Hypothesis" seems unlikely and ridiculous;it isn't impossible if one can define what the computer ismthe program is and the operator of the computer is.. Still it is the opinion of this author that this theory is based on out new technology based on computers and computer software and would have been unheard of in the 1970's or 80's and would have been laughed our of the scientific profession so many Physicisits would still like askance at this theory.

THE TWO DIMENSIONAL UNIVERSE

THE TWO DIMENSIONAL MODEL BASED ON THE YANG BAXTER RELATION IS BASED ON A PAARTITION FUNCTION OF A TWO DIEMSNIONAL LATTICE FOR WHICH ELLIPTICAL JOSEPHSONVORTICIES ACT AS FLAT MATTER WITHIN A VIBRATING MATRIX OF PHOTONS TRAPPED WITHIN BOSOEINSTEINIAN CONDENSATE AT JUST ABOVE ZERO DEGREES KELVIN. THE EQUATION $Z=n\{\exp[-E(n)/kT$ where E(n) is the energy of the Nth state of matter, K=Boltzman Constant and T=temperature in degrees kelvin. The Free Energy (F)=-kT ln Z and Z is defined abpve. The Boltzman equation relates to energy states at phase transitions as in the latent state of freezing or mLf and of vaporization as mLv. At absolute zero there is a confluence of vibrating photons trapped in a matrix accounting for the mass gap in Yang Mills Theory and as mentioned previously in this book. The correlation functions between spins or isospins can be lbelled *σi and σj revealing criticality seeking behavior as the metric g ij regarding parameters of crit??? initial and j the final event. This expreession is g ij $=< σiσj > -< σi >< σj >$ and depends on the distance separating the states explained by the variable xwith regard to th???*

Distance and explains "Spooky Action at a Distance" as x approaches infinity as a distance between the states. $g\ ij`x^-$ $\dfrac{\tau e^{-x}}{\zeta}$ *where ζ = correlation length and τ relates to relative time as* x is the distance between states. As the cor???

Elation length approaches infinity we have a phase transition ind in any phase of flat matter such as Elliptical Josephson Vorticies the temperature of the system can vary as there are 252 discreet states of matter in any active black hole. These states under superpressures included radiation which is flat matter in states such as liquid, solid BosoEinsteinian Condensate and would neatly fit as Elliptical Josephson Vorticies fitting into the vortex of space-time as it constricts toward zero as the event horizon of any active black hole is approached. This is one reason why a hologram or flat matter is imprinted at the event horizon in terms of microdata and evaporates or dissolves into space-time as microdate over a 360 degree area as well as via Hawking Radiation spuming outward from the event horizon. Basically these data are super-compactified into a two dimensional state where the other dimensions are super-compactified into a Super-brane while the two macroscopic dimensions can be viewed like a stop action photograph. The Ising Model has an energy operator as $\epsilon n = \sigma n \sigma n + 1$ *at criticality and reveal conformal invariance whereby the relation to conformral*

Field theory has a !:1 association with the fields of the Ising Model.

APPENDIX

BRANES; A STRING IS A one-BRANE WHICH COUPLES TO A BACKGROUND SECOND DEGREE TENSOR. Zero-branes are ten dimensional building blocks for space in the pre-Big Bang epoch. The second degree tensor is purported of negligible mass as indicated by the ZERO-BRANE. THE SOURCE OF THE BACKGROUND SECOND DEGREE TENSOR IS R uv where the integral of D to the d power of x where x is the string or one-brane in D dimensions applies to R u v g u v where g u v is the metric acting on R u v for the zero-brane with respect to x which is the one-brane. R u v is the second degree tensor upon which the metric g u v acts. In four dimensions a monopole is dual to two electrons acting on a zero-brane. In 10 dimensions a string is analogous to a five-brane based on p-brane potentials. This involves dual fields such as a tensor R=R* from Ra1...a n=R8b1...b n.p-branes are encircled by a hypersphere which relates to M theory being compactified (curled up) by a circle for type IIa strings. The charge of a p-brane is based on $Q = \int *$
R from limit S d – p – 2 for electric charges and $Q \int_{Sp+2} R$ *for electromagnetism..P – branes tie in with the potential involved with permutations of a field tensor. p brane tensors a*

Are associated with a tensor of the pth rank R a1...a p and electric and magnetic charges can be associated with p-branes with superalgebra.

Dzero-branes represent the vacuum state. ALTHOUGH INDICATED AS ten dimensional building blocks of space they actually are zero-dimensional. ONE-BRANES REPRESENT STRINGS WHICH ARE TWO DIMENSIONAL OR POSSIBLY ONE DIMENSIONAL. If all the dimensions in a system or universe are conserved such that the total number of dimensions are constant;then zero branes would have to be ten dimensional in the vacuum state. Six dimensions for CalabiYau Manifolds and four dimensions of space-time. As the "c" boundary is approached infinite mass with reducing length and width occur when length becoming infinite. In this case width and height approach zero but do not reach it and become infinitely small curled up and compactiifed. In general although showing duality between different systems which are abelian membranes are described by the forces involved with mass or energy associated with the membrane with reference of n-dimensional space where n dimensions would have n-1membranes or n-1 brane.

FLAT OR MINTKOWSKI SPACE IS DESCRIBED MATHEMATICALLY AS THE LINE ELEMENT OR ds2=dx2+dy2+dz2-c2dt2. FLAT SPACETIME IS SPACE-TIME WITHOUT ANY CURVATURE IN OTHER WORDS A VACUUM STATE HERE R g a b=0 which indicates that the space-time curvature metric=0 and therefore gravity =0 in the vacuum state. CURVED SPACE-TIME IS GENERALLY DESCRIBED BY ds2=ek| r|(dx2+dy2+dz2-c2dt2)+dr2 where r=space-time curvature metric described by tensor as R g a b. R g a b or r is determined by the inertial mass of the object doing the curving and the curving is performed by bosons and possibly gravitons or fermions. Spiral space-time has k=-i(the square root of-1)to the n cotangent theta power as suggested by Dr. Roger Penrose and proposed by this author.

MANIFOLDS
THE SIMPLEST MANIFOLDS ARE CARTESIAN SPACES WHERE A MANIFOLD STRUCTURE OR SURFACE IN TERMS OF TOPOLOGIES

IS R to the d power with what's called an identity map Rd implies R d. The coordinate functions of this map are cartesian coordinates. If coordinates are a I; R d is the manifold of the standard Cartesian coordinates. a i=ax+ay+az and R to the d power is the tolological expression of the standard manifold or the Cartesian Coordinate system. If a manifold is imbedded in another manifold it is a submanifold. On a string basis submanifolds can be orbifolds or Calabi Yau manifolds which are submanifolds for spiral manifolds for asymptotically flat but curved space-time on a macrostatic surface which is expanding and simultaneous rotating as at black hole event horizon. RIEMANNIAN CURVATURE A RIEMANNIAN SPACE IS THE SPACE COORDINIZED BY xi(power)with a fundamental form of the Riemannian Metric g I jdx I dx j where g=(g ij) obeys the metric tensor. g is of differentiability class C2(all second order partial derivatives of g I j exist and are continuous. g is symmetric g I j=g ji;g is nonsingular |g I j| doesn't equal 0. The differential form and distance from g isn't variant with regard to changes in coordinates.

R I j k l=g I ir(Rr superscript with jkl as a subscriptwhere R jkl with ias a superscript is the Riemann tensor of the second kind. The Riemann Tensor of the first kind is R I j k

$$= \frac{\tilde{A}jki}{xk} - \frac{\partial \tilde{A}jki}{xi} + \Gamma ilr\Gamma jk \text{ with r as a superscript} + \Gamma ilr\Gamma jk \text{ with r as}$$

a superscript-$\Gamma ikr\Gamma ji$ with r as a superscript. **Here**

Γ *is a Christoffel symbol or the derivatire of a tensor. Above is*

$Rijkl- \frac{\tilde{A}jki}{xk} - \frac{\partial \tilde{A}jki}{xi} + \Gamma ilr\Gamma jk$ with r as superscript-$\Gamma ikr\Gamma jl$ withr

as superscript. Skew Symmetrys involve Bianchi^' sIdentity R ijkl+Riklj+Riljk=0 skew symmetry is R i j k l=-Ri j kl an d second skew symmtery is R ijkl=-R i j l k with R j k l with i as superscript=-R j l k withi as a superscript. Block symmetry is R i j k l=R k l i j. These symmetry properties must fir with the

$n2(n2- \frac{10}{12}$ *COMPONENTS OF THE RIEMANN TENSOR(R i j k l)where the diagnal tensor without s. PTR.*

Rijkl=g I iRjkl is subscript and I as superscript in the diagonal metric te tensor calculations for the Riemann Metricgives six cases R one R 212 and 1 R 313 and 1 R 323 and 1 R 213 and 1 R 232 and 1 R 123 and 1 which proves with the partial derivatives of the Christoffel symbols of tensors according to the previous formulas give R I j k l=0 for all I j k and l indicatin the summation of all Riemann forces and space is zero. The math of all these combinations is very difficult to reproduce by typing.

BIBLIOGRAPHY

1. Peat, F. David. Superstrings and the Search for the Theory of Everything. Yang Mills Forces p.114
2. Kaku, Michio. Strings, Conformal Fields and M theory. Ising Model p.176-78
3. Wald, Robert. General Relativity. Chicago, Ill. University of Chicago Press.1984 4. CPT THEOREM; Quantum Field Theory Kaku, Michio
4. Metric tensor(General Relativity)Wikipediaa and Spacetime. en.m.wikipedia.org.spiral Space-time Einstein 1912 Fractal Time. p.108-109 Braden, Gregg 2009 Library of Congress HAWKING RADIATION. Wikipedia
5. Peat, F. David. Superstirngs and the Search for the Theory of Everything. p.106-107. Calabi Yau Manifolds
6. Kaku, Michio. Quantum Field Theory. Renormalization Actions in Quantum Field Theory
7. Peat, F. David. Superstrings and the Search for the Theory of Everything.
8. Kay, David C. Tensor Calculusp.129 Osculating Plane
9. Kaku, Michio. Strings, Conformal Fields and M theory.
10. Peebles, P.J.E. Principles of Physical Cosmology. p
11. Chang, Alan. HAMILTON JACOBI EQUATIONS UNIVERSITY OF CHICAGO 2013. Zeno's paradox: The Math Forum at Drexel University
12. Tipler, Frank j. The Physics of Immortality

13. Godel, Kurt. Godel's Incompleteness Theorems
    en.m.wikipedia.org
14. Randall, Lisa. Warped Passages
15. Green, BrianThe Elegant Universe. and Wick, Mitchell
    Albert. Megaphysics, A New Look at the Universe.
16. Kay, David. CTensor Calculus.
17. Kaku, Michio. Strings, Conformal Fields and M Theory.
18. Wikipedia.Electronen.wikipedia.org/wiki/Electron
19. Spooky Action at a Distance Quantum Entanglement
20. Wikipedia. Or en.wikipedia.org/wiki/Quantum
    entanglement
21. Hau, Len. Harvard Research circa 2003.

BIBLIOGRAPHY

Barrero, John D. The Anthropic Cosmological Principle. Oxford England. Oxford Press.1986

Brade, Gregg. fractal Time 2009 Library of Congress.

Greene, Brian. The Elegant Universe. NewYork. Vintage Books editor Random Press.1999

Hawking, Steven and Penrose, Roger. The Nature of Space and TimePrinceton, N.J;Princeton Science Library 1996

Kaku, Michio. Quantum Field Theory. A Modern Introduction. Oxford university Press.1993

Kaku, Michio. Strings, Conformal Fiels, and M theory 2nd edition. Springer Press.2000.

Kay, David C. Tensor Calulus Schaum's Outline Series.

N.Y.McGraw Hill 1998.

Peat, F. David. Superstrings and the Search for the Theory of Everything. Chicago. Contemporary Books 1998

Peebles, P.J.E. Principles of Physical Cosmology. Princeton Series in Physics. Princeton University Press 1993

Wald, Robert m. General Relativity. Chicago, Illinose. University of Chicago Press 1984

Wikipedia: on lin encyclopedia.

Randall,. Lisa. Warped Passages HarperCollins

Publishers. N.Y.2005

Tipler, Frank J. Physics and Immortality. Anchor Books division of Random House.1993

GLOSSARY

Abelian: equations having a coefficient or variety in a specific group, g, algebraic number fields, tensors of the same degree or cohominy group

Anisotropic: not isotropic, lacking observational symmetyry

Anti-symmetric: tensors or vectors that are equal but opposite and can therefore partially cancel or cancel

Aymptotic: that which approaches a level or degree but never reaches it;asymptotic flatness appears without curvature but doesn't reach it

Bianchi's Identity: The identity of groups of Riemannian 4 space that is antisymmetric and Abelian and cancels each other out of being equal but opposite

"The Big Bang" A theory proposed describing a Friendman type I open expanding f;at universe with is homogeneous and isotropic

"The Big Swirl" A Big Bang with a progressively decreasing rotational vector from an infinite curvature point of space-time to asymptotic flattness

Black Hole: collapsed matter from a neutron star or galaxy with extreme curvature of space-time at the central nexus due to extreme gravity of of the spiral space-time

Calabi Yau Manifold: a surface which represents a relative isotropic portion of spacetime with a puckering to accommodate multiple dimensions considered a twisted variant of the orbifold

Choas: absolute disorder

Chiral: a mirror image or absolute symmetry

Closed string: a two or one dimensional building block of matter from energywith movements in 10 or 26 dimensions without breaking the string

Compactified: when every point of the dimensions are curled up mathematically making the size approach zero. First determined by Kaluza and Klein

Conformal Space: when every point in space relative to every other point maintains its relative position regardless of what the space is doing

Dark Matter;an indirectly measured mass causing perturbations in gravity(the curvature of space-time)caused by mass. Acts as cosmic glue containing possibly baryonic particles and neutrinos

Event Horizon: area where a black hole is perceived by measurementsEntropy: degree of disorder

Entropy: degree of disorder
Ex nihilo: out of nothing

M(Membrane)theory: the 5 dual string theories into one massive theory of everything which incorporates membranes which vibrate and incorporate all energy and matter

Isoropic: observational symmetry

Geodesic: a unit of space-time

Gravity: the curvature of space-time caused by mass;actually an effect not a force

Membranes: a description of matter in terms of energy states with stress energy densities described in the number of states with regard to dimensions

N;number of dimensions in N dimensional space

Open string: a two or one dimensional bulding block of matter with movements in a multidimensional plane

Orbifold: space-time manifold in an open twisted cone configuration utilized in string theory

Relativity: the behavior of matter and energy with regard to other matter and energy;energy and space have a different vantage point from other matter and energy including stress energy, time and mass with changes regarding relative velocity

RicciTensor: that tensor which represents inertial mass or resistance against pull or push

Riemann Forces: all strong and weak forces in nature

Riemannian Space: Mintowski space with Riemann curvature of space-time caused by mass. Flat space if no mass is present

Scalar: the magnitude compone t of a vector or tensor with regard to direction

Six dimensional string manifold: curled up closed strings in configuration according to Kaluza and Klein which is 10-33 cm and may be Calabi Yau Manifolds

S=rθ the equation of arc length when applied to the osculating plane will pptro an infinite number of dimensions. The unit tangent vector of a sphere of 2 π *radians in motion is 2 π R cosθ where θ is π radians. The sphere travels at HOR THE HUBBLE* EXPANSION FACTOR. *As θ approaches zero cos 0 appraches 1 causing space – time to approach –* $\frac{1}{2e}$ *– i times the number of dimensions where e = 2.71828 then spacetime =* $-\frac{1}{2}e-$ *i(to the n power)x1 where n approach* $\dfrac{es\infty\frac{or1}{-1}}{2ei\infty}$ *power or 0 which indicates that n infinite number ???*

Down to theta approaches zero causes r or the arc length at the circumference to approach zero

R ijkl -   R ji=-8πG e (ij, ji) =g
 kl ji

-8πG e(ij, ji)=g ji

$\quad$ vector product of Rij   'Rji=e(ij, ji) cos π =-e(ij, ji)
$\qquad$ 8πG = Λ -1 is from cos θ $\theta = \pi$ klR ij. R ji ji for space-time curvature from antiparticle of metric g ji on antiparticles Rji kl=contra-variant tensor kl on covariant tensor ji ji is from antiparticle g ji kl is from gravity of contra-variant tensor for metric g ij for matter

$\quad$ Ijkl=antigravity effect on particles from antiparticles

$\quad$ 2
$\quad$ R ij Rji   2   2
---------------------------. e ji where Rij Rji$/\left\|R^{\ ij}\right\|\left\|R^{ji}\right\| = \cos \quad \theta$

$\quad$ 2
$\left\|R^{ij}\right\| \qquad \left\|R^{ji}\right\|$

add e kl to e ij e kl = R kl / $\left\|\begin{smallmatrix} Rkl & Rkl \end{smallmatrix}\right\|^2$ 'g kl   cosθ 'g kl=-1. g kl where $\theta = \pi$ radians as covariant tensor For contravariant tensor e kl = R kl squared / $\left\|\begin{smallmatrix} Rkl & Rkl \end{smallmatrix}\right\|$ .g $-$ g kl = g lk$\|$

kl

R ijkl = g kl/g ij'gkl =-$8\dfrac{\pi G}{-16\pi G}=\dfrac{1}{8\pi G}$ whioch is the reciprocal of the cosmologic constant $\wedge$ $8\pi G$ =6.67x10 $\dfrac{11}{8\pi}=7.5x10$ 10 joules – seconds which is a huge antigravity effect of Dark Energy from the antimatter antimatter e???

The gravitational coupling constant k=---$8\pi G/c4$ ---$8\pi G/c$ 4 is also synonymous with antigravity between 2 particles of matter or anti---matter. As matter--- matter interactions have a positive gravity anti---matter anti---matter interactions are antigravity Q.E,D.

Using E=mc2 with the number of strings I the quantum bubble for antimatter and matter being the mass the calculation emerges as E=7.5x 10 10 joules(3x10 10 cm/sec)2=6.75x10 31 joule---sec or on one second 6.75 x10 31 joules as the blast force from "The Big Bang" ;as antigravity is the predominant blast force Dark Energy blasted out in the 360 degree Orb Blast producing 750 billion galaxies from the Mas string calculation. Note 10 31 is 10 to the thirty---first power

NOTE: Although some sources list the cosmologic constant (Λ) as $\frac{4}{8\pi G / c}$ this has no impact on the mathematical calculations only labeling. Other sources list this as the gravitational coupling constant. G is in kg---meters/sec 2 6.67x10 11/8π =7.5 x 10 10 for number of strings. Calculation or at 10 7 erg per joule for 'Big Bang' blast force is e=mc 2 or e(joules)=7.5x1 10(3 x 10 10)2=75 x 10 30 joules or at 10 7 erg per joule 75 x 10 37 erg or 7.5 x 10 38 erg